CIRCULATION OF THE BLOOD
THE CIRCULATORY SYSTEM
for Young Scientists

Name _____ Date _____

PURPOSE
Learn about your blood and how it takes
care of all the parts of your body.

HOW TO USE THIS LEARNING GUIDE: You can use this learning guide to study on your own. Just read a step, do it, and check It off. Then you can go right on to the next step!

Do each step in order without skipping around.

When you complete a section, check in with your teacher and show them your work.

A. BLOOD CELLS

☐ READ: *Circulation of the Blood*, page vi, Your Young Scientist Journal.

☐ ACTIVITY: Get a *Young Scientist Journal,* a notebook you like, or make a science journal of your own.

    ❏ If you want, write on the inside "Circulation of the Blood" or "How My Blood Works" or whatever you want.

    ❏ Think of, and write down in your journal, some ways you would like to use it.

☐ READ: *Circulation of the Blood*, Chapter 1 Cells.

☐ ACTIVITY: Look at a prepared slide of onion cells with a microscope (If a microscope isn't available, look at pictures of onion cells.)

1

☐ ACTIVITY: In your science journal, make a drawing showing how a living thing is made of cells. Label what it is. Share it with another person.

☐ READ: Chapter 2 Your Blood to the heading "White Blood Cells."

☐ ACTIVITY: Look at a prepared slide of red blood cells with a microscope. (If a microscope isn't available, look at pictures.)

☐ READ: Chapter 2, section "White Blood Cells."

☐ ACTIVITY: Look at pictures of white blood cells.

☐ READ: Chapter 2, section "Platelets."

☐ ACTIVITY: Look on your own body or a friend's for a scab to see platelets doing their job.

☐ READ: Chapter 2, section "Making New Blood Cells" to the end of the chapter.

☐ ACTIVITY: In your journal, draw a picture of each part of the blood and what It does.

> ☐ red blood cells ☐ white blood cells
>
> ☐ platelets ☐ plasma
>
> ☐ Label each one and share them with your teacher.

_____

Teacher check in

B. BLOOD CIRCULATION

☐ READ: Chapter 3 Your Blood Vessels to the heading "Working Together."

☐ ACTIVITY:

> ☐ Use objects to show the jobs these blood vessels do:
>
> - arteries
> - veins
> - capillaries

❑ Use objects to show why some blood is bright red and other blood is dark red.

☐ READ: Chapter 3, section "Working Together."

☐ ACTIVITY:

❑ Look at a preserved animal specimen that has been injected with dye to show arteries and veins. (If a preserved animal is not available, look at a color picture of an animal that shows arteries and veins.)

❑ Find at least one artery and one vein.

☐ READ: Chapter 3, section "One More Important Player."

☐ ACTIVITY: In your journal, make a drawing that shows the difference between the blood in an artery between the heart and lungs, and the blood in an artery between the heart and another part of the body. Label it. Share it with another person.

☐ READ: Chapter 3, section "Two Important Blood Vessels—Well, Actually Three."

☐ ACTIVITY:

❑ Point to the right side of your heart and then the left side of your heart.

❑ Use your finger to trace on your body a possible path of your blood from

- the right side of your heart to your lungs,

- back from your lungs to the left side of your heart,

- to your aorta,

- to smaller arteries in some part of your body,

- then back through your veins to your vena cava to the right side of your heart,

- and then to your lungs.

_____

Teacher check in

C. YOUR HEART

☐ READ: Chapter 4 Your Heart, to heading "The Two Sides of Your Heart."

☐ ACTIVITY: Do the What's Your Heart Rate? activity on page 39.

○ Show your teacher.

☐ READ: Chapter 4, section "The Two Sides of Your Heart."

☐ ACTIVITY: Use objects to show each of the steps of blood moving through the upper and lower chamber of a heart.

☐ READ: Chapter 4, section "How It All Works."

☐ ACTIVITY: Find "Your Heart and Lungs Worksheet," attached to the back of this learning guide. Using red and blue pencil or marker, make arrows to show carbon-dioxide blood and oxygen blood flowing through the heart and lungs. Try to do this without looking at the book illustrations.

☐ ACTIVITY: Do the Round and Round It Goes activity on p. 40 with another person.

○ Show your teacher.

☐ READ: Chapter 4 section "One Last Thing."

☐ ACTIVITY: Find the coronary arteries and veins on a plastic heart model. (If you don't have a plastic model of a heart, look at a color picture of a heart.) Show them to another person and explain how the heart muscle is fed and gets rid of its wastes.

☐ ACTIVITY: Use a plastic model of a heart, or a color picture of a heart. Label these parts on the model or picture, or point them out to your teacher:

☐ aorta	☐ pulmonary artery to right lung
☐ upper vena cava	☐ pulmonary veins from right lung
☐ lower vena cava	☐ pulmonary veins from left lung
☐ coronary arteries	☐ pulmonary artery to left lung
☐ coronary veins	

Note: Some models do not show well the arteries and veins that are attached to the heart. If your model shows where a blood vessel attaches to the heart but not the vessel itself, just label or point out where the blood vessel should attach to the heart.

_____
Teacher check in

D. WORKING WITH OTHER BODY SYSTEMS

☐ READ: Chapter 5 Working with Other Systems to the heading "Digestive System."

☐ ACTIVITY: Use objects to show someone else how the circulatory system interacts with the respiratory system.

☐ READ: Chapter 5, section "Digestive System."

☐ ACTIVITY: Use objects to show someone else how the circulatory system interacts with the digestive system.

☐ READ: Chapter 5, section "Excretory System."

☐ ACTIVITY: Use objects to show someone else how the circulatory system interacts with the excretory system.

☐ ACTIVITY: Do the Find the Parts! activity on p. 51.

_____
Teacher check in

E. PUTTING IT ALL TOGETHER

☐ ACTIVITY: Add some notes to your journal about what you've learned about the circulatory system, questions you might want to explore, or anything else you want to put in your journal before you move on to your next science adventure.

☐ READ: Chapter 6 Putting It All Together.

☐ ACTIVITY: Do the Put It All Together activity on page 55.

_____
Teacher check in

YOUR HEART AND LUNGS WORKSHEET

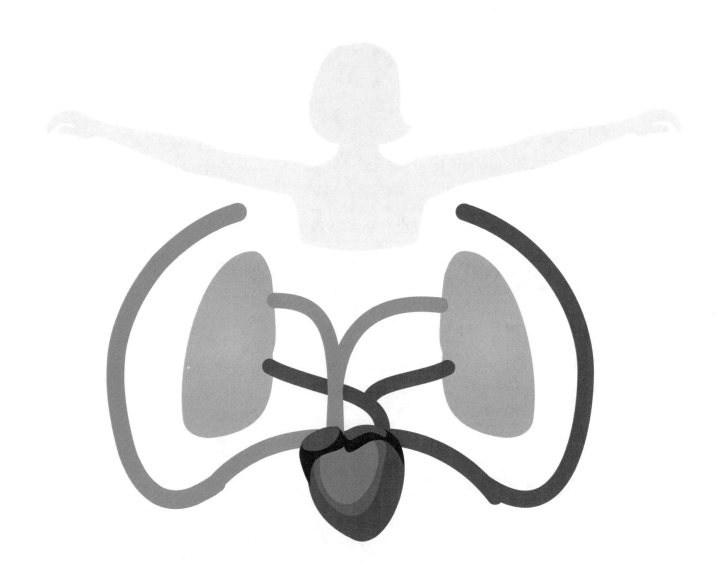

I completed

CIRCULATION OF THE BLOOD

THE CIRCULATORY SYSTEM
for Young Scientists

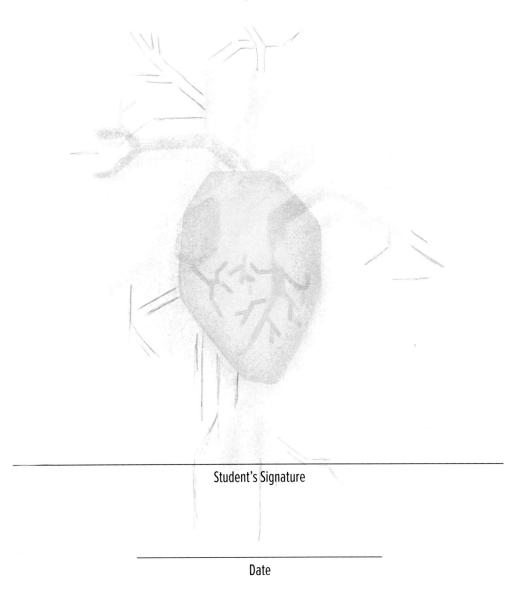

_____
Student's Signature

_____
Date

CIRCULATION OF THE BLOOD

THE CIRCULATORY SYSTEM
for Young Scientists

CIRCULATION OF THE BLOOD

THE CIRCULATORY SYSTEM
for Young Scientists

HERON BOOKS

Published by
Heron Books, Inc.
20950 SW Rock Creek Road
Sheridan, OR 97378

heronbooks.com

————————————

Special thanks to all the teachers and students who
provided feedback instrumental to this edition.

————————————

ISBN: 978-0-89-739242-6

Printed in the USA

6 September 2022

At Heron Books, we think learning should be engaging and fun. It should be hands-on and allow students to move at their own pace.

To facilitate this we have created a learning guide that will help any student progress through this book, chapter by chapter, with confidence and interest.

Get learning guides at
heronbooks.com/learningguides.

For teacher resources,
such as a final exam, email
teacherresources@heronbooks.com.

We would love to hear from you!
Email us at *feedback@heronbooks.com.*

Your
YOUNG SCIENTIST JOURNAL

Scientists love to explore the world and how things in it work. They like to go new places and discover things they've never seen before.

They also like to keep track of what they find. They often fill books with notes and drawings of what they see, and include their thoughts and questions about it. These books are called *science journals*.

What's fun about a science journal is that you can use it to draw pictures or sketches of things that interest you. You can write down ideas you have about things, make maps, write down questions you have and things you want to find out more about. You might even stick in it samples of things you find—flowers, bugs, leaves, feathers, spider's webs—who knows what?

Young Scientist

JOURNAL

The learning guide that goes with this book will sometimes ask you to look at things and make notes or drawings in a journal of your own.

Whatever you put in your science journal, it will be full of your own personal discoveries. No two journals are alike.

You can use a journal like the one shown here, or you can use a notebook of your choice. You might even want to make your own science journal and use that.

Whichever type of journal you choose, it will be a place to keep drawings and notes about what you are finding out about the world and how it works.

So get ahold of a science journal, or make one, and then get going to see what you can find out. Who knows what might be waiting for you?

IN THIS BOOK

CELLS

A FAMOUS SCIENTIST

Almost four hundred years ago, long before cars and planes existed, even before the United States became a country, there lived an English scientist named Robert Hooke. From a young age, he loved experimenting and inventing things.

In fact, he spent his whole life observing, experimenting and inventing. He especially liked to invent things that would help him do more observing and experimenting.

At age 30, he became interested in observing the microscopic world. He wanted to see the tiny parts of things that we can't see with our eyes, things we can only see with a microscope. To do this, he had to improve the type of microscope being used at that time.

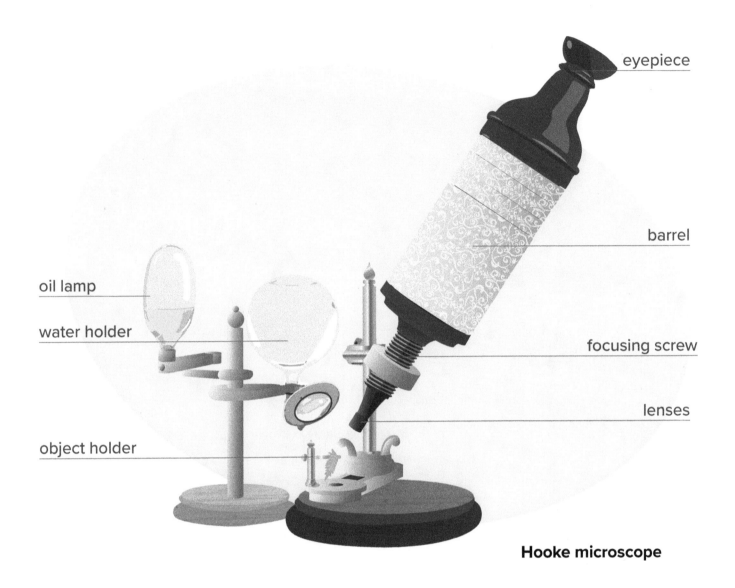

Hooke microscope

eyepiece

barrel

focusing screw

lenses

oil lamp

water holder

object holder

When Robert Hooke was a boy, a microscope was really just a plaything. It had two **lenses** (pieces of curved glass that magnify things) inside a tube. It was fun to use it to look at small things and see them look larger.

But he wanted to see much smaller things. So he experimented and designed a better microscope. It used three lenses and had a light that shined through the object being viewed.

Using his new microscope, he soon made an exciting discovery.

He found every living thing he looked at under his microscope seemed to be made of small shapes that looked like little rooms. Another word for a small room is "cell." So when he wrote a book about what he saw through his new microscope, he called these little shapes **cells**.

He had discovered the smallest part of every living thing. And every scientist after him used the word he had chosen.

Robert Hooke went on to create many more inventions and make many more discoveries. But this book starts off with this one, exciting discovery.

All living things are made of cells!

MILLIONS AND MILLIONS

Cells are so small, there are millions and millions of them in every living plant and animal.

Your little toe is made of more than a billion cells. That's a thousand million, or 1,000,000,000 cells!

Not only that, there are many different kinds of cells.

When you look at human cells through a microscope, you can see how different they can be from one another.

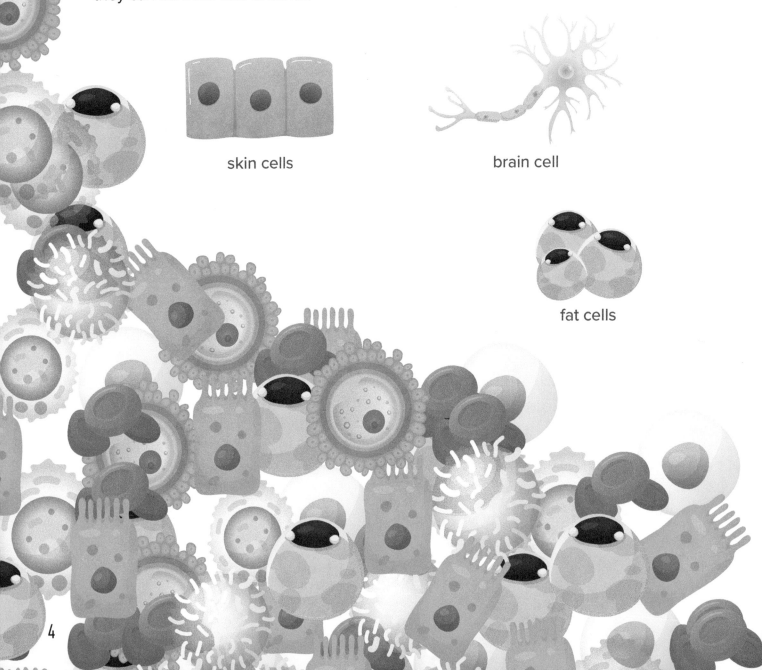

skin cells

brain cell

fat cells

THEY'RE ALIVE

Even though cells are so tiny you can only see them through a microscope, they are alive. They live and die just like the animals and plants they are part of.

Cells need food and water to survive. This comes from the foods you eat and the liquids you drink.

Oxygen is part of the air you breathe. Every one of your cells needs oxygen to stay alive. That's why you spend your whole life breathing air into your lungs. It's to provide oxygen for your millions and millions of cells.

Your cells use food, water and oxygen to help you grow, and to make it possible for you to move around and do things. And when they use oxygen, food and water, your cells also make a little bit of heat. With millions and millions of cells making heat, your body stays warm.

Every cell grows, then makes more of the same kind of cell by dividing in two. We call a full-grown cell a **parent cell**, and this divides into two identical, but smaller, **daughter cells**. This is how your body grows. Every cell, once grown, turns into two, and your body makes about a billion new cells every hour. That's about 25 billion new cells each day!

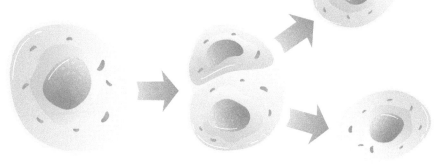

GETTING RID OF WASTES

Whenever a human or animal eats or drinks, its body takes what it needs to stay healthy and then gets rid of what isn't useful. We call these things a body can't use **wastes.** When you use the bathroom, you are getting rid of your body's wastes.

Your body's cells work the same way. After they use food, water and oxygen, they get rid of the leftovers they can't use, which we call wastes.

Some liquid wastes are collected as **urine**, the yellow liquid your body gets rid of when you go to the bathroom. Another liquid waste is sweat.

The air you breathe out has cell waste in it too. How does that work?

As you know, the air you breathe has oxygen in it. When your cells use oxygen, they put out a leftover waste called **carbon dioxide**. What you breathe out has a lot of carbon dioxide in it.

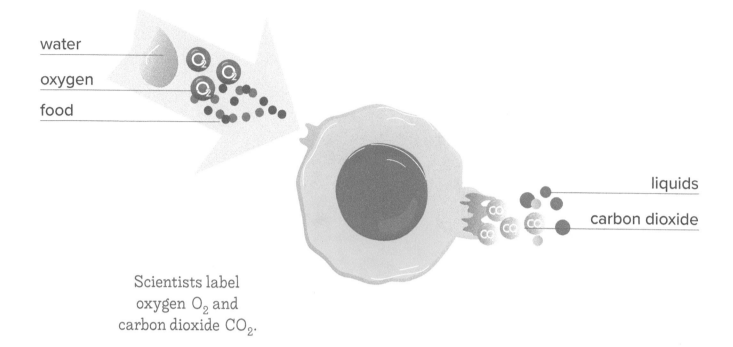

water

oxygen

food

liquids

carbon dioxide

Scientists label
oxygen O_2 and
carbon dioxide CO_2.

Every time you breathe in and out, you are feeding your cells oxygen and getting rid of carbon dioxide.

Like all living things, cells die. While millions of new cells are being made, millions of cells are also dying.

And that adds one more thing to our list of wastes—dead cells. If you have ever noticed tiny flakes of dead skin coming off your body, you were looking at millions of dead skin cells!

YOUR BLOOD

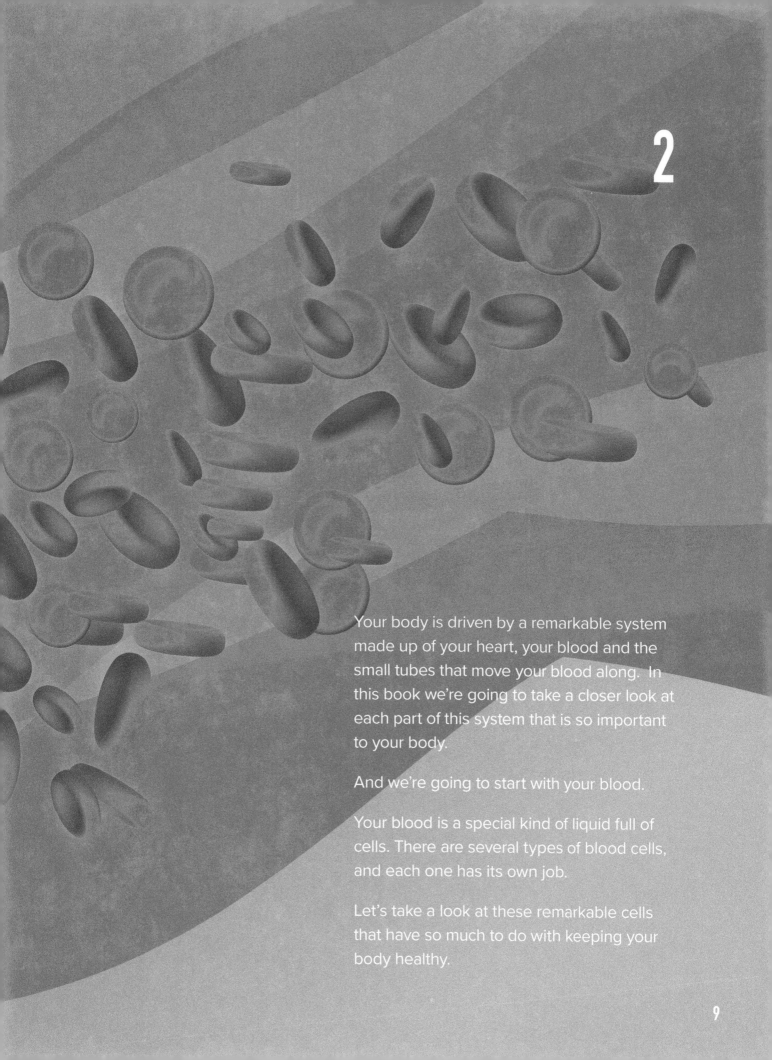

2

Your body is driven by a remarkable system made up of your heart, your blood and the small tubes that move your blood along. In this book we're going to take a closer look at each part of this system that is so important to your body.

And we're going to start with your blood.

Your blood is a special kind of liquid full of cells. There are several types of blood cells, and each one has its own job.

Let's take a look at these remarkable cells that have so much to do with keeping your body healthy.

RED BLOOD CELLS

Let's start with your **red blood cells**. These are actually pink, but when millions of them crowd together, as they do in a drop of blood, they make your blood look red.

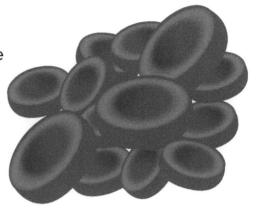

Scientists often call these RBCs (**R**ed **B**lood **C**ells) for short.

Under a very powerful microscope, each red blood cell looks like a tiny round raft.

Your red blood cells do an important job. They pick up from your lungs the oxygen your cells need, and carry it through tubes called **blood vessels** (VES ulz) to the rest of your body. Your red blood cells help keep all your other cells alive!

They use the mineral iron to help them hold on to the oxygen they carry. If you've ever seen iron, this might seem odd. It's true that **iron** is a heavy metal that was used in the past for tools and weapons. Today you might see it used in making fences and frying pans.

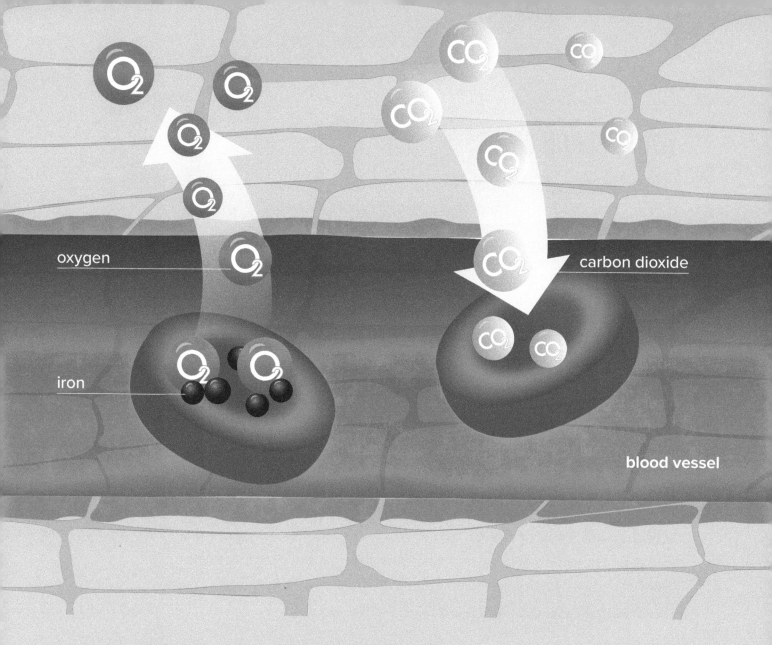

oxygen

iron

carbon dioxide

blood vessel

But iron in a very tiny form is also found in many foods we eat, like eggs, meat, beans and leafy green vegetables. In this tiny form it does some important jobs in the body. One of these is helping red blood cells grab hold of oxygen.

So, with the help of iron, your red blood cells pick up oxygen and carry it to cells throughout your body. When a red blood cell delivers its bit of oxygen to a cell, it also picks up a bit of carbon dioxide waste and carries it back to your lungs for you to breathe out.

Each one of your millions of red blood cells is working all the time, picking up a bit of oxygen, carrying it to a cell, and carrying a bit of carbon dioxide away. It then does the same thing again, over and over and over, day after day after day. That's pretty remarkable, don't you think!

WHITE BLOOD CELLS

Did you know that your body has many other tiny living things inside it? These are called **bacteria** (bak TEER ee uh). They can only be seen with a microscope.

Maybe you've heard that bacteria are bad because they make you sick. Well, let's see if that's true.

Almost all bacteria are smaller than the cells in your body. You have about ten times as many of them in your body as you have cells!

That brings up this question. If all bacteria are bad, how does your body stay alive? The answer is pretty simple. Most bacteria are actually good for you! In your stomach, for example, millions of bacteria help you digest your food. Without their help, your cells would have nothing to eat.

But there are a few bacteria that can cause trouble, giving you a sore throat or upset stomach, even causing cavities in your teeth. And you have other very tiny things inside your body called **viruses.** They might cause a cough, an earache, a fever, or a cold.

bacteria

The difference between viruses and bacteria are that viruses are usually much smaller, and many bacteria are good while most viruses definitely are not. Most bacteria help your body. Only a few bacteria can make you sick, but many viruses can make you sick.

Sometimes people use the word *germ* to talk about viruses *and* the few bad kinds of bacteria that can make you sick.

virus

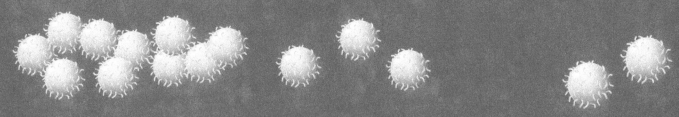

Here's the good news. Your blood has an army of fighters which can beat almost any germ that finds its way into your body. The soldiers in this army are your **white blood cells**, or WBCs for short. Their job is to protect your body from germs and harmful bacteria while leaving the good bacteria alone.

There are millions and millions of soldiers in your WBC army. And when your body gets sick or injured, it quickly makes extra white blood cells to help you get better.

There is something about white blood cells that makes them different from other cells in your body. They can move around on their own! They do this by sprouting hundreds of tiny legs that help them crawl along to get to the spots in your body that need them. Scientists also think they use these legs to sense where and how to move, so that they can crawl to an area that needs help.

Most of the time the white blood cells simply travel along in your blood as it moves through your body. Some attack germs that might have gotten into your blood. Others travel to damaged or sick areas of your body. When they get there, they use their legs to hold on to the walls of your blood vessels to keep from being swept away by your blood as it flows along.

Then these white blood cells leave your bloodstream. Squeezing out between the cells of your tiniest blood vessels, they crawl to the area where cells are sick or damaged. Once there, they "eat" germs and any dead cells by surrounding them and swallowing them up.

It's good to know you have an army of germ fighters in your blood, isn't it?

PLATELETS

There is another type of useful cell in your blood. These go to work when you start to bleed from a scrape or cut in your skin.

Have you ever wondered why the bleeding eventually stops? Why doesn't it just go on bleeding?

When you get a cut or scrape, it may cut into one of the blood vessels beneath your skin and blood flows out. Fortunately, blood vessels have a way to close themselves to stop the bleeding.

Platelets (PLAYT lits) are the blood cells that come to the rescue when one of your blood vessels is damaged. They clump together to form a plug where the blood vessel was cut to stop the blood from flowing out.

This little plug is called a **blood clot.** The blood clot gradually turns into a **scab**, a hard protective coating where the injury was. The scab protects your body while it heals. It keeps you from bleeding more, and it keeps germs out. Depending on how deep and large the cut is, new skin will grow within a few days to a week. At that point, the scab has done its job so it falls off.

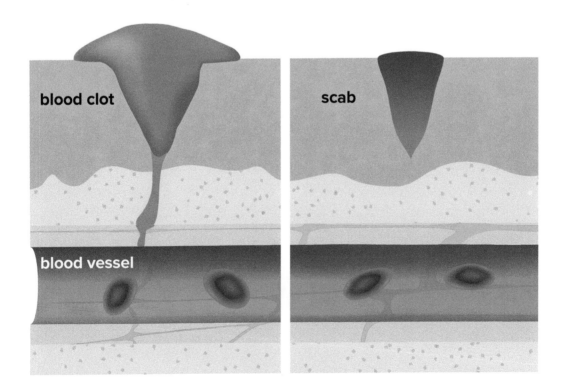

blood clot

scab

blood vessel

Sometimes you can get hurt without cutting your skin. For example, you might bump into something hard. This can cause a **bruise**, where some of your blood vessels break and bleed *underneath* your skin. Just like with a cut on your skin, your platelets come to the rescue to stop bleeding under the skin.

Bruises often change as they heal. A bruise might look pink or red for a day, then purple or black and blue for a few days. As more and more healing occurs it might look green, then turn yellow or brown as the healing completes. When the bruise is gone, this means the area is fully healed.

With your platelets there to help, most bruises, cuts and scrapes will disappear completely, leaving your body as good as new!

A tip to help you recover more quickly from a bruise is to put a plastic bag of ice wrapped in a towel on an injured area for 15 minutes, then wait half an hour and do the same thing again. This will help stop blood flowing from any broken blood vessels beneath your skin.

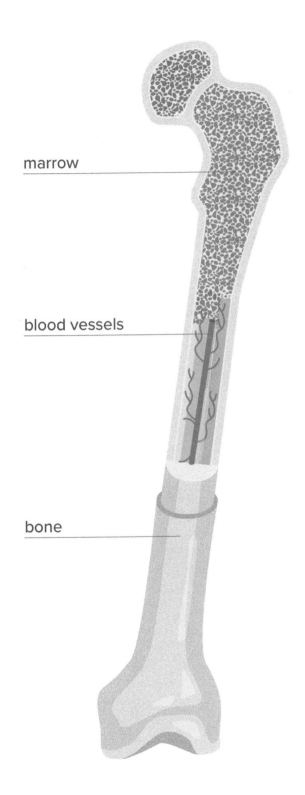

marrow

blood vessels

bone

MAKING NEW BLOOD CELLS

Believe it or not, your blood cells wear out and die, so your body needs a continuous supply of new ones. You might be surprised to learn that new blood cells are made inside your bones!

Your bones are hard and whitish on the outside. On the inside, however, they are soft and red. The soft inside part of your bones is called **marrow**, and this is where new blood cells are made.

If you break open the leg bone of a chicken, you'll see that inside it's partly hollow, but has a soft, red layer of marrow. Human bones are very similar.

Your bone marrow makes new red blood cells, white blood cells and platelets.

When some of your red blood cells get old, your body breaks them down and saves the iron in your bone marrow.

This iron is reused. It's placed in new red blood cells, and these are moved into your blood through super-tiny blood vessels found in your bones.

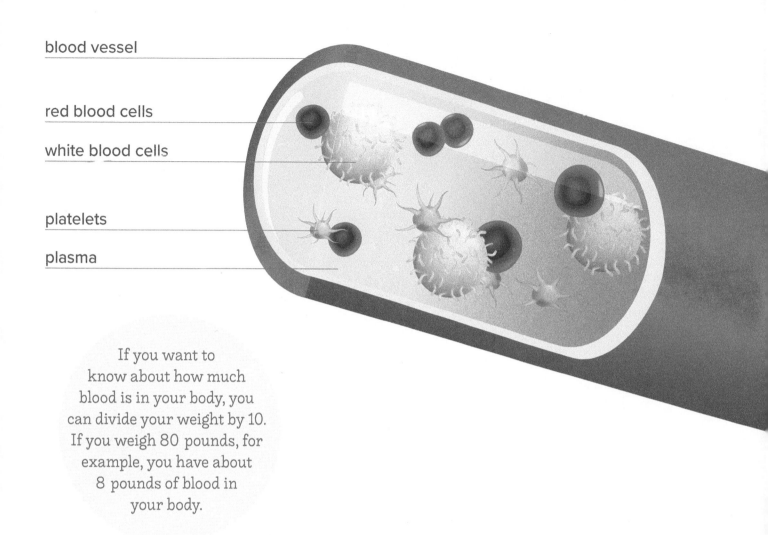

blood vessel

red blood cells

white blood cells

platelets

plasma

If you want to know about how much blood is in your body, you can divide your weight by 10. If you weigh 80 pounds, for example, you have about 8 pounds of blood in your body.

PLASMA

All the different kinds of blood cells travel around your body in a golden-yellow fluid called **plasma** (PLAZ muh). Plasma, which is mostly water, is the main ingredient in your blood. It carries your blood cells to the places they are needed. It also takes food, water and minerals to your cells, and it carries away wastes.

Red blood cells, white blood cells, platelets and plasma—this is what your blood is made of.

Normally, there is a gallon or more of blood flowing through your blood vessels. That's a lot of blood! And it's a good thing, because your cells couldn't live without it!

YOUR BLOOD VESSELS

WHAT IS CIRCULATION?

Now that you know something more about your blood, it's time to talk about the blood vessels that carry it along and take it where it's going.

When something **circulates**, it starts somewhere and flows around in a pattern like a circle, ending up back where it started. **Circulation** of the blood is what happens when your blood flows around and around through your body. It flows through your heart to all the different cells in your body, then flows back to your heart and then to all your cells again. It just keeps flowing around and around.

Blood travels in a system of blood vessels that go to every part of your body. They make it possible for your cells to get what they need to live.

There are large vessels, medium-sized ones, small ones, tiny ones—and as you learned in the last chapter, even super-tiny ones inside bones.

In the center of this system of blood vessels sits your heart, pumping away day after day, pushing your blood through your blood vessels.

Your heart, blood vessels and blood cells, all working together, are called your **circulatory** (SUR kyoo luh tor ee) **system.**

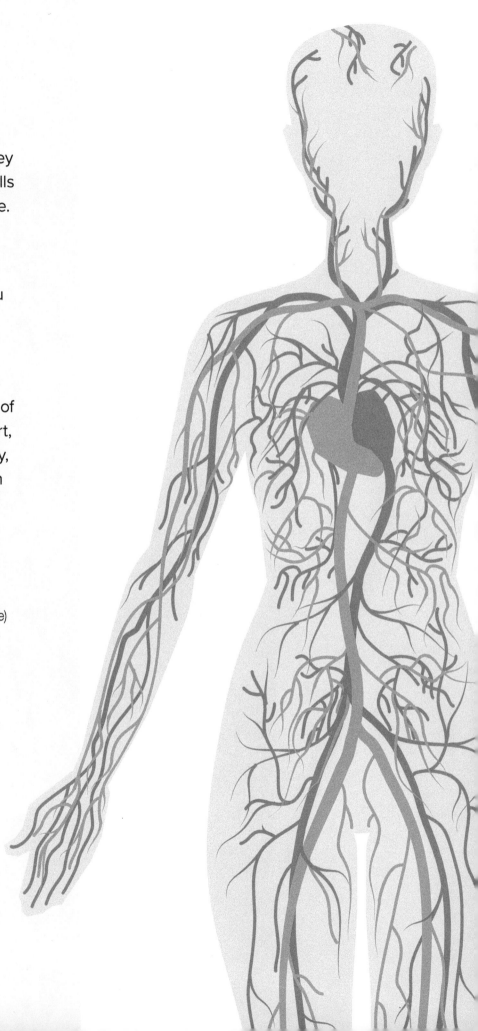

THREE TYPES OF BLOOD VESSELS

When people talk about blood vessels, they sometimes just call them "veins."

But scientists and doctors have special names for three different kinds of blood vessels. Each one does a particular job, and only one of them is actually a vein.

Let's start with your blood vessels that do the job of carrying blood *away from* your heart. These are called **arteries** (AR tuh reez).

Your arteries carry blood freshly full of oxygen from your heart to your cells. Blood full of oxygen is bright red. In drawings of the circulatory system, you will often see many blood vessels colored red and many that are blue. The red blood vessels are arteries.

Veins are the second type of blood vessels. These bring blood *back to* your heart from your cells. The blood they carry is full of carbon dioxide, the leftover waste after your cells use oxygen. Your heart will send this to your lungs so you can breathe it out.

In drawings of the circulatory system, veins are usually colored blue. The blood in your veins isn't really blue. It's red, just not bright red like the blood in your arteries. (Blood full of carbon dioxide is very dark red. But veins look blue when you see them beneath your skin).

The last group of blood vessels are your **capillaries** (KAP uh lair eez). These are tiny blood vessels only one cell thick that connect your thinnest veins to your thinnest arteries.

How thin is a capillary? It is 100 times thinner than a single strand of hair on your head! So thin that your red blood cells have to move through them single file!

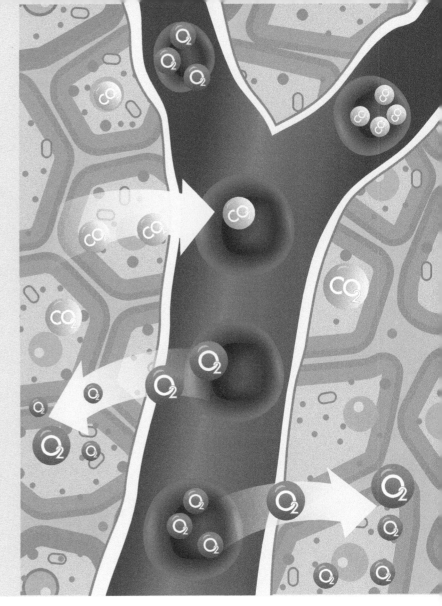

Capillaries help your blood cells connect with the trillions of other cells in your body. Capillary walls are so thin that the oxygen carried by the red blood cells can pass through them to get to your cells, and your cells' carbon dioxide waste can pass the other way to get to the red blood cells.

After they drop off oxygen and pick up carbon dioxide, the red blood cells flow through the capillary into a vein, and are carried back to your heart.

When white blood cells need to get to an area that needs protection from invading germs, they are able to squeeze through the capillary walls, then crawl to the infected area.

Amazingly, there are so many blood vessels in your body that if you laid them all out, end to end, they would be over 60,000 miles long. That's long enough to circle the world more than twice!

That's a *lot* of blood vessels in a single human body!

WORKING TOGETHER

As you have probably noticed, your heart and your blood vessels work as a team.

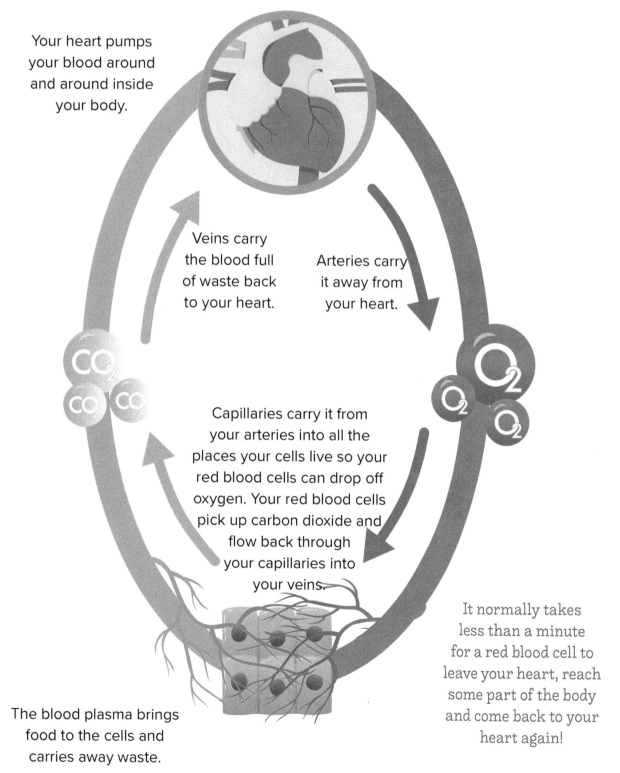

Your heart pumps your blood around and around inside your body.

Veins carry the blood full of waste back to your heart.

Arteries carry it away from your heart.

Capillaries carry it from your arteries into all the places your cells live so your red blood cells can drop off oxygen. Your red blood cells pick up carbon dioxide and flow back through your capillaries into your veins.

It normally takes less than a minute for a red blood cell to leave your heart, reach some part of the body and come back to your heart again!

The blood plasma brings food to the cells and carries away waste.

Let's look at how this whole exchange works, using your arm as an example.

A single artery, full of blood with oxygen and food, runs down each of your arms, splitting into two at the elbow.

Millions and millions of tiny capillaries connected to these arteries take the blood to your cells so the oxygen and food can be dropped off and the carbon dioxide and other wastes picked up.

The capillaries then connect to a vein that carries the blood with the wastes back to your heart.

Working together, your heart, blood vessels and blood keep all your cells alive and well.

oxygen food water

carbon dioxide waste

ONE MORE IMPORTANT PLAYER

We've talked about your blood cells, blood vessels and heart. But we haven't talked yet about how the oxygen you breathe gets into your blood, and how the carbon dioxide waste from your cells gets out of your body. This is, of course, where the lungs come into play.

Your **lungs** are a pair of organs filled with air that sit inside your chest. They are important players in the circulatory system, and they work closely with the heart in doing their job. This is why your heart and lungs are right next to one another, and this is where things get interesting!

As you know, your arteries carry oxygen and your veins carry carbon dioxide. But there are some special arteries and veins connecting your heart and your lungs that do just the opposite.

Special veins carry fresh oxygen from your lungs to your heart so it can be pumped around your body to your cells. They are called veins because, like all veins, they carry blood *toward* your heart.

Special arteries carry carbon dioxide from your heart to your lungs so it can be breathed out. Again, they are called arteries because, like all arteries, they carry blood *away* from the heart.

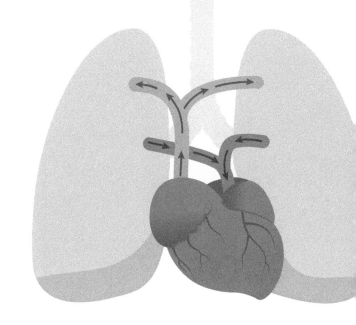

Although your lungs are part of your breathing system, the way your lungs and heart work together shows how different systems in your body often help one another do their jobs.

TWO IMPORTANT BLOOD VESSELS—
WELL, ACTUALLY THREE

When red blood full of oxygen arrives in your heart, it is ready to be pumped to all your cells. To get it there, your heart pumps it into your largest artery, called the **aorta** (ay OR tuh). About an inch wide, your aorta comes out of the top of your heart. It has three large arteries that branch off for the upper body. It then curves down to run along your backbone, gradually getting narrower and narrower.

Your aorta ends where it divides into two smaller arteries that go to your legs. Along the way many arteries branch off it, carrying blood full of oxygen to all the different parts of your body.

Once it has visited your cells, your blood flows back toward your heart through a similar group of veins. Smaller veins feed into two large veins that empty blood full of carbon dioxide into one side of your heart. Each of these veins is called a **vena cava** (vee nuh KAY vuh). One comes from the upper body, called the **upper vena cava**. One comes from the lower body, called the **lower vena cava**.

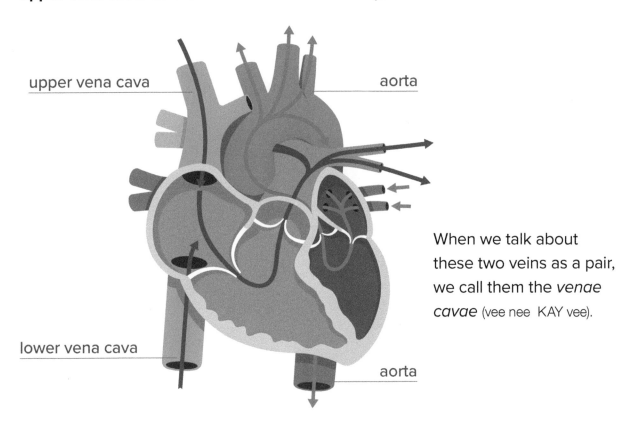

upper vena cava

aorta

When we talk about these two veins as a pair, we call them the *venae cavae* (vee nee KAY vee).

lower vena cava

aorta

Here we see these important
vessels with the rest of the
circulatory system. Notice that the
lower vena cava runs along the
backbone next to the aorta.

Your heart and all your blood
vessels—arteries, capillaries and
veins—form a complete system
which circulates your blood
around and around.

upper vena cava

arteries

veins

heart

capillaries

aorta

lower vena cava

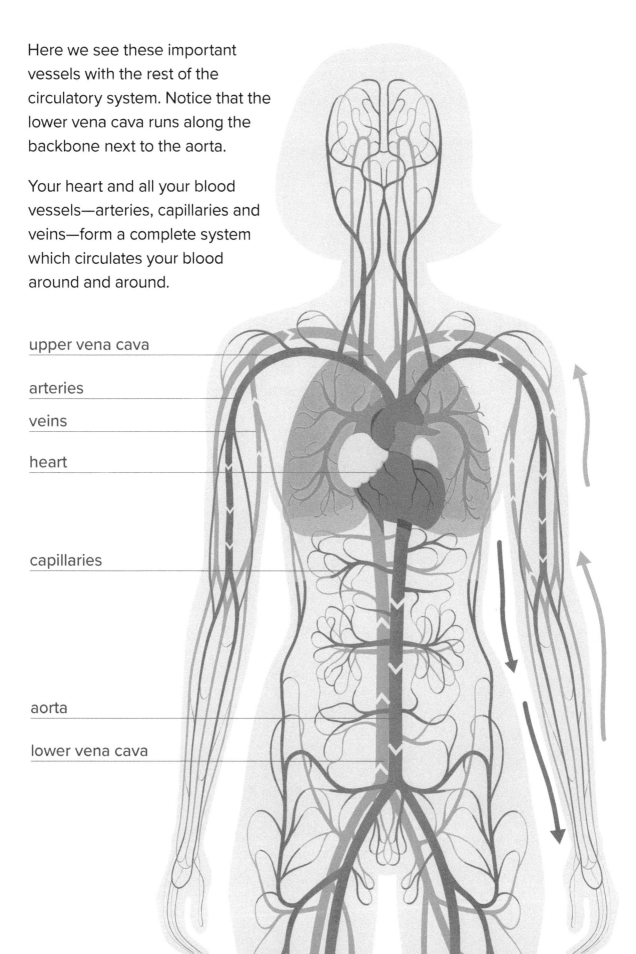

YOUR HEART

4

The organ called your **heart** is the remarkably strong muscle that drives your circulatory system. Over and over again, many times every minute, this muscle pumps blood to all parts of your body, keeping your cells alive and fed.

LUB-DUB, LUB-DUB

Your heart was one of the first parts of your body to form and start doing its job. It started beating long before you were born, so that by the time you entered this world it was already a strong muscle that had been working for months.

Each time your heart beats, it pumps blood to the rest of your body. And, remarkably enough, it beats seventy, eighty, ninety, or even a hundred times every minute.

Using an instrument called a stethoscope, a doctor can hear clearly the *lub-dub, lub-dub, lub-dub* sound your heart makes when it beats.

When it is quiet, you might be able to hear (or feel) your own heart beating inside your body: *lub-dub, lub-dub, lub-dub*.

HEART RATE

What we call **heart rate** is how many times a person's heart beats in a minute. Your heart rate shows how hard your heart is working. If your heart is beating 100 times a minute, it's working a lot harder than when it's beating 50 times a minute. It's pumping twice as much blood to the rest of your body.

To measure your heart rate, we measure how many times it beats in a minute. How do we do that?

It's actually pretty easy. As your heart pumps again and again, this causes a steady beat. We call this steady beat your **pulse**. There are a few places on your body where it's easy to feel this steady beat. One is on the inside of your wrist, the other is on the side of your neck. At these spots, it's easy to count how many times your heart beats in a minute. In other words, it's easy to measure your pulse.

To check your own heart rate, feel your pulse and count the number of beats in a minute. You can also count the number of beats in 15 seconds and multiply that by four.

A normal heart rate for an older child or adult is usually between 60 and 100 beats per minute. Sometimes it will be faster, sometimes it will be slower, depending on what the person is doing.

For example, if you ran full speed for a minute, your heart rate would go up. Why? It's because your cells use oxygen to create energy. Without enough oxygen, your cells run out of energy. So, when your muscles work hard, your heart works hard also to give your muscles more oxygen. If you took a nap, your heart rate would slow down. There is not as much oxygen needed for that!

It all depends on how much oxygen your cells need. The more you use your muscles to lift things, jump, run or dance, the more oxygen is needed by those muscle cells. When you are relaxing, your cells don't need as much oxygen.

Every person has their own heart rate. Young children normally have higher heart rates than teens and adults. Well-trained athletes often have bodies that work so well that their normal heart rate is low. Their hearts are stronger, so they pump more blood with each beat. Some well-trained athletes have a heart rate between 40 and 50 when they are resting.

Just like other muscles, you can train your heart and make it stronger by being very physically active or doing lots of exercise.

THE TWO SIDES OF YOUR HEART

Your heart is a muscular organ made up of two pumps that work together. One side of your heart (sometimes called your **left heart** because it is towards the left side of your body) receives blood full of oxygen from your lungs and pumps it to the rest of your body.

The other side of your heart (sometimes called the **right heart** because it is towards the right side of your body) receives the blood full of carbon dioxide cell waste that has been returned from the rest of your body and pumps it to your lungs.

Each side has two sections, called the **upper chamber** and the **lower chamber**. (A **chamber** is an enclosed space, like a room.) These chambers fill up with blood, then empty, fill up, then empty, over and over.

Each chamber of your heart has a tiny door that opens when the chamber is full, and shuts after the blood in it has been pushed out. These little doors are called valves. A **valve** is something that starts and stops liquids by opening or closing. When you turn on a water faucet, you are opening a valve inside the faucet so water comes out. When you turn it off, you are closing the valve and the water stops.

The valves in your heart only open in one direction. Your blood is always getting pushed forward by the beating of your heart, and this is what opens a valve. Once a valve is pushed open, some blood flows into the next chamber and the valve flaps shut. This keeps the blood from flowing back where it came from.

This is how your blood always moves through the four chambers of your heart in a certain exact pattern. Let's start with your right heart.

1.   Blood flows into the right upper chamber.

2.   When it is full, the blood pushes open a valve between the upper and lower chambers.

3.   The blood then pours into the lower chamber, and the valve shuts.

4.   When your heart beats, it squeezes the full lower chamber. This pushes the blood through another valve, this one leading to an artery that goes to your lungs. *Whoosh.* Out goes the blood from the lower chamber into the artery, and the valve shuts.

You'll notice in diagrams of the heart that the left heart is shown on the right side of the diagram, and the right heart is shown on the left side of the diagram. That's because when you look at it from the front, the sides are reversed.

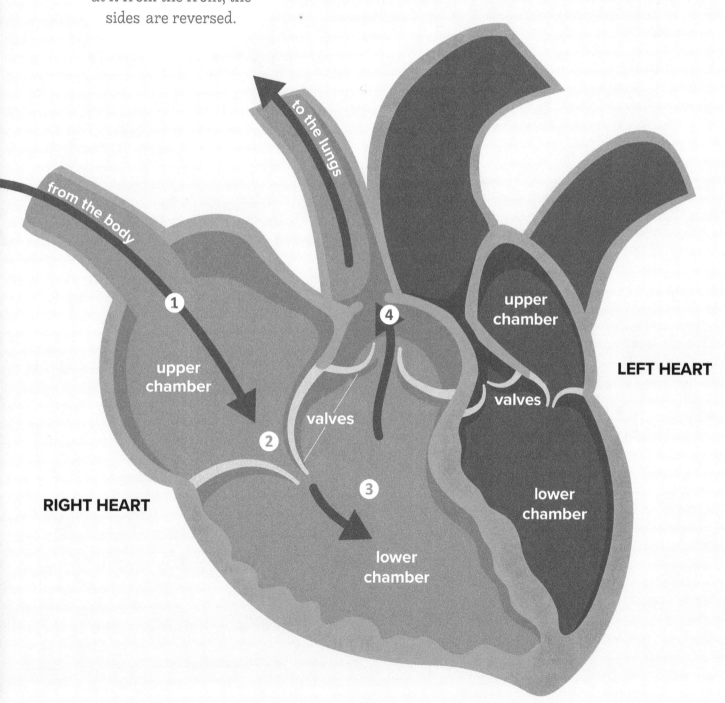

to the lungs

from the body

1

upper chamber

4

upper chamber

LEFT HEART

valves

2

valves

3

RIGHT HEART

lower chamber

lower chamber

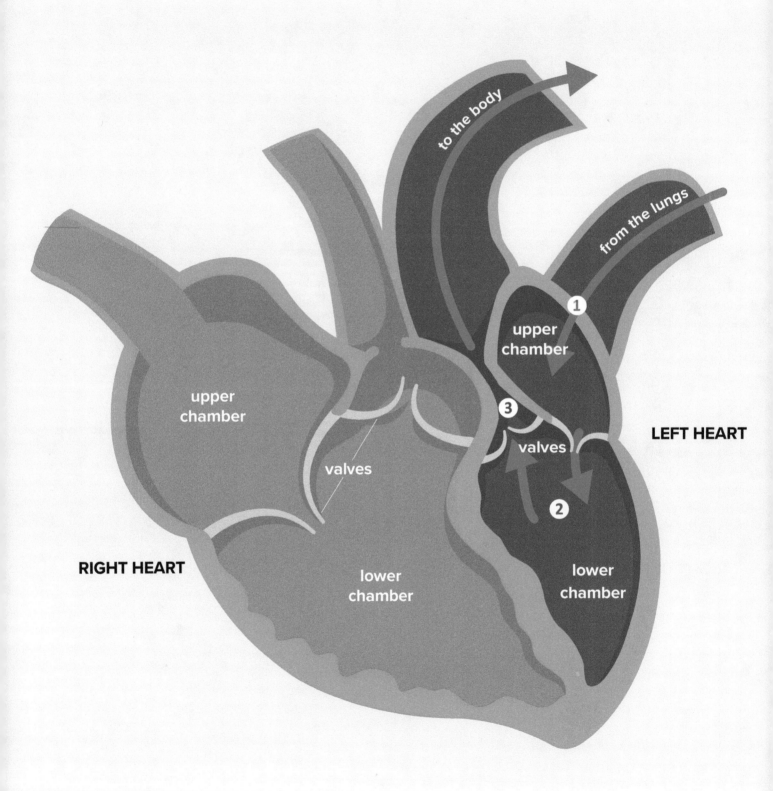

to the body

from the lungs

① upper chamber

③

② valves

LEFT HEART

lower chamber

upper chamber

valves

RIGHT HEART

lower chamber

After this, your heart relaxes, some more blood flows into the upper chamber, and you're back at the first step again.

The left side of your heart works in a similar way.

1. Coming from your lungs, blood full of oxygen flows into the left upper chamber.

2. When the chamber is full, this pushes open the valve between the upper and lower chambers. The blood pours into the lower chamber and the valve shuts.

3. Your heart beats, squeezing the lower chamber, and the blood gets pushed out through another valve into your aorta. From there it travels to all parts of your body.

Meanwhile, new blood has filled the upper chamber again. And over and over it goes.

So, what is the lub-dub sound you can hear when you listen to your heart through a stethoscope? It's the sound of the valves shutting. Every *lub* is the sound of the two valves between the upper and lower chambers closing. Every *dub* is the sound of the valves from the two lower chambers closing.

You can think of the upper chambers as the *receiving* chambers. That's where blood comes in. And the lower chambers are the *pushing* chambers. That's where blood goes out.

So, *lub-dub, lub-dub, lub-dub* is a bit like the heart saying, *"in-out, in-out, in-out."*

HOW IT ALL WORKS

1. Your right heart pumps blood with carbon dioxide to your lungs through two arteries called pulmonary (PUL muh nair ee) arteries. **Pulmonary** means "having to do with the lungs." You'll notice the pulmonary arteries are colored blue, not red like other arteries. Can you figure out why? It's because they carry carbon dioxide. But they are still arteries because they carry blood away from the heart.

2. The carbon dioxide enters your lungs so you can breathe it out, and your blood picks up oxygen.

3. Blood with oxygen returns to your left heart through four **pulmonary veins** (two from each lung). Even though they are red, they are veins. Why? That's right, because they carry blood to your heart!

4. Oxygen-rich blood enters the left upper chamber.

5. It flows into the left lower chamber.

6. It is pumped out through the aorta to arteries and capillaries for all the cells in your upper and lower body.

7. Blood with carbon dioxide returns from the cells through veins, entering the right upper chamber through the upper vena cava and lower vena cava.

8. It flows into the right lower chamber.

And we're back at step 1 where your heart pumps the blood to the lungs to get rid of the carbon dioxide and pick up some fresh oxygen.

It takes only half a minute for your blood to do all that, to move from your right heart to your lungs, back to the left heart, to your body and back again to your right heart.

This repeats over and over. And this is how your blood circulates around and around, never stopping, always feeding your cells.

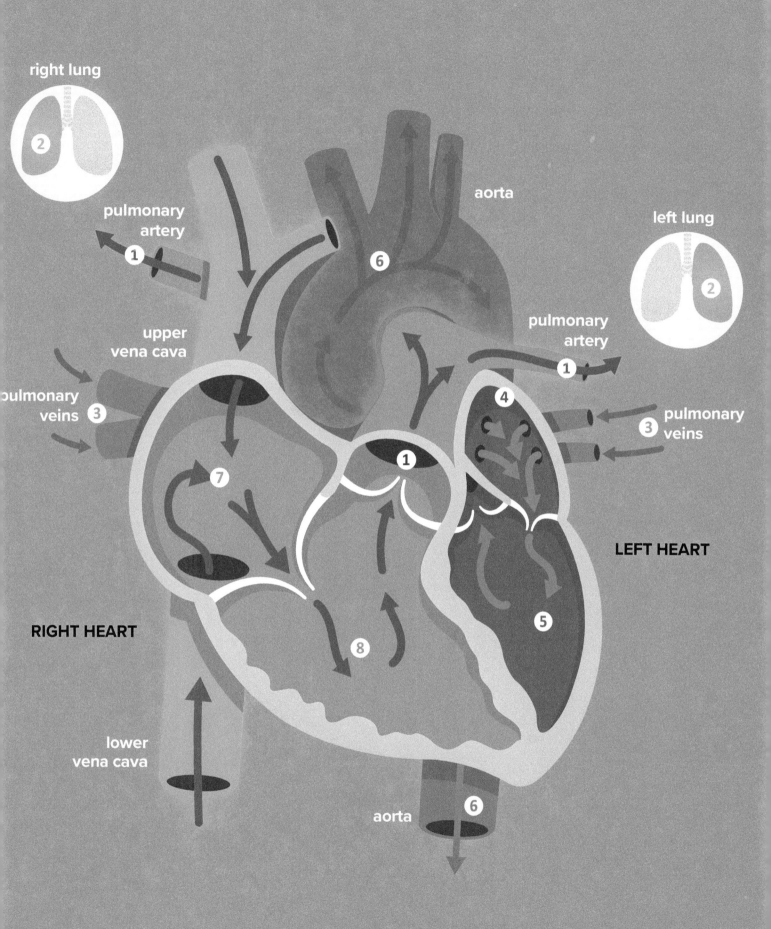

right lung

pulmonary
artery

aorta

left lung

pulmonary
artery

upper
vena cava

pulmonary
veins

pulmonary
veins

LEFT HEART

RIGHT HEART

lower
vena cava

aorta

37

ONE LAST THING

Your heart is a muscle and it's working all the time. Doesn't it need oxygen and food also?

Yes, it does.

The heart muscle has two arteries and two veins of its own. These are called **coronary** (KOR uh nair ee) **arteries** and coronary veins. "Coronary" means "having to do with the heart."

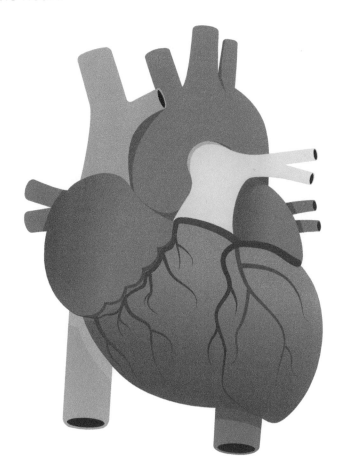

So with every beat, your heart is pumping blood to itself too!

From months before you were born, and continuing on throughout every minute of every day, the remarkable muscle we call your heart will keep on pumping, sending blood through your entire body, keeping it healthy and alive.

WHAT'S YOUR HEART RATE?

Let's Do This!

For this activity you will need

- a timer that shows seconds.

Steps

1. Feel your pulse and count how many times your heart beats in a minute. You can also count the number of times it beats in exactly 15 seconds and multiply by 4. This is your heart rate.

2. Run in place for one minute, then take your pulse again. What is your heart rate now? Is there a difference?

3. In your science journal, describe what happened to your heart rate and what might have caused this.

Let's Do This!

ROUND AND ROUND IT GOES

For this activity you will need

- a piece of drawing paper at least 3 feet long.

- 6 small red buttons labeled "O_2" for oxygen

- 6 small blue buttons labeled "CO_2" for carbon dioxide

- one larger button, any color, labeled "RBC" for red blood cell

- red and blue pencils or markers

Steps

1. Make a 3 foot drawing like the one on the next page.

2. Label all the parts and color them.

3. Use your drawing and your RBC button to show how a blood cell would travel from the lower body to the upper body and back again to the lower body.

4. Now you will use your drawing to show how oxygen and carbon dioxide travel around in the body.

5. Start by putting the RBC button in the lower body. Then put three red O buttons in each lung, three blue CO_2 buttons in the upper body, two blue CO_2 buttons in the lower body, and one blue CO_2 button on the RBC button.

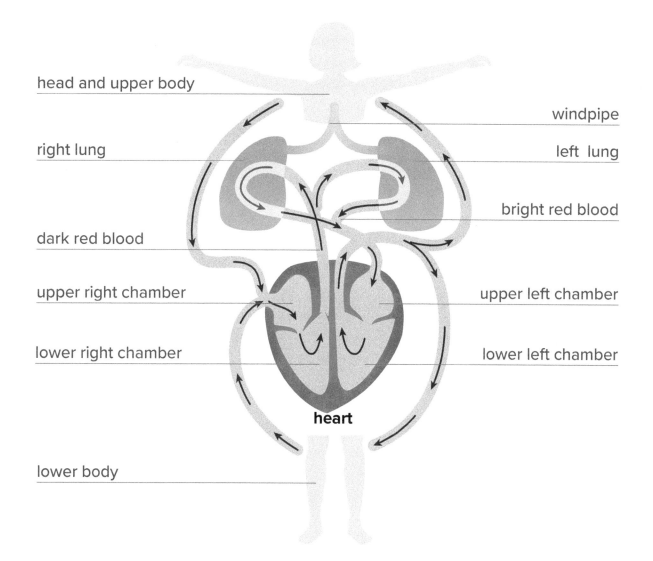

head and upper body

windpipe

right lung

left lung

bright red blood

dark red blood

upper right chamber

upper left chamber

lower right chamber

lower left chamber

heart

lower body

6 Show another person how the RBC gets to the upper body and back to the lower body, picking up and dropping off oxygen and carbon dioxide in the correct places.

Two things to remember:

- The RBC always carries either oxygen or carbon dioxide.

- Oxygen cannot travel in the RBC when carbon dioxide is there and carbon dioxide cannot travel in the RBC when oxygen is there.

WORKING
WITH OTHER
SYSTEMS

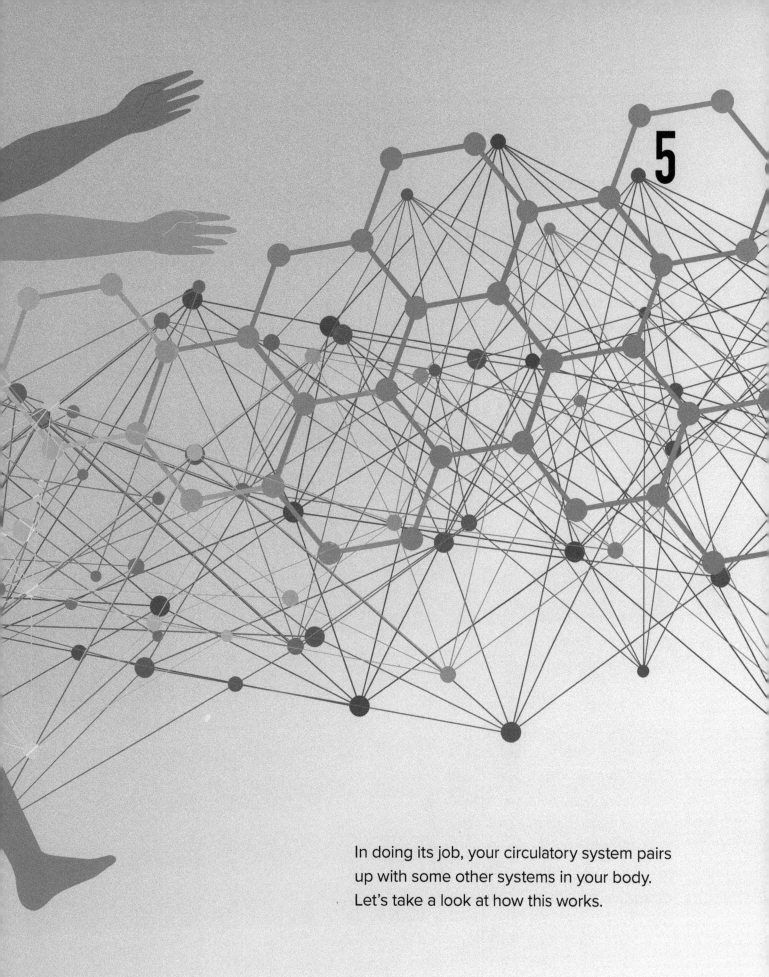

5

In doing its job, your circulatory system pairs up with some other systems in your body. Let's take a look at how this works.

RESPIRATORY SYSTEM

Your **respiratory** (RES pruh tor ee) **system** is how your body takes in the oxygen it needs. Your lungs are the most important part of this system. When you breathe in, they take oxygen from the air and when you breathe out they get rid of carbon dioxide waste.

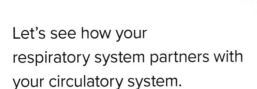

Let's see how your respiratory system partners with your circulatory system.

When you breathe in through your nose and mouth, air fills up many tiny air pockets in your lungs called **alveoli** (al VEE uh lye). These have lots of capillaries wrapped around them, and this makes it easy for the oxygen you breathe to pass into your blood where it is picked up by your red blood cells.

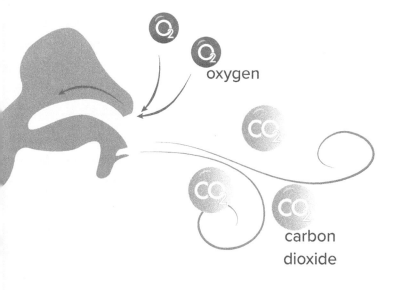
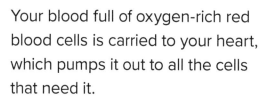

oxygen

carbon
dioxide

Your blood full of oxygen-rich red blood cells is carried to your heart, which pumps it out to all the cells that need it.

The oxygen passes into your cells, and there it helps produce energy. Then carbon dioxide waste needs to be taken away from the cells.

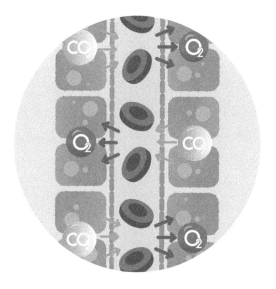

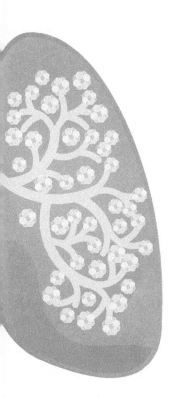

Your red blood cells do you a favor by picking up this carbon dioxide waste and carrying it back to your lungs. Then you breathe out, and this gets rid of the carbon dioxide.

When you breathe in, you take in more fresh oxygen and the whole sequence happens again. And again...and again!

Working together, these two systems constantly take in oxygen and get it to all your cells and pick up carbon dioxide and get rid of it.

DIGESTIVE SYSTEM

Your cells are happy when you eat a salad, a hamburger, an apple or an avocado because they need the healthy things inside. But first the food needs to be digested, or broken down into microscopic size. Imagine your blood trying to carry a piece of apple to your cells. It's way too big!

What does your body do to break down the food you eat into something your blood can carry and your cells can use?

The system that makes the food you eat useful to your cells is called your **digestive** (dye JES tiv) **system**. Let's see how this works.

Let's say you're going to eat a slice of cheese pizza. Once you've chewed it up and swallowed, your pizza ends up in your **stomach,** where it is mixed with juices that break it down into even smaller pieces. Then it moves from your stomach into your **small intestine** (in TES tin) where it's broken down even more. By now your pizza is kind of a soupy mush. As the mush passes through your small intestine, food your cells can use is picked up by your blood and carried to your **liver**.

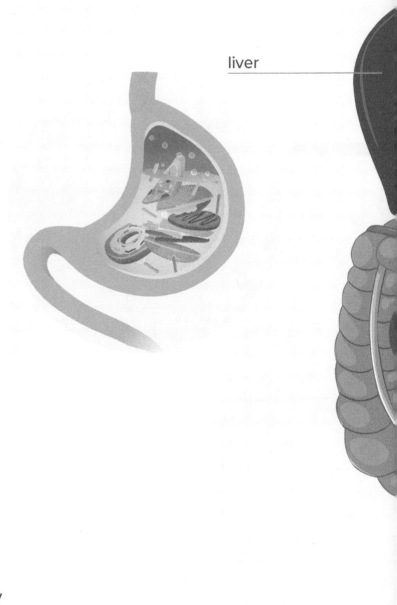

liver

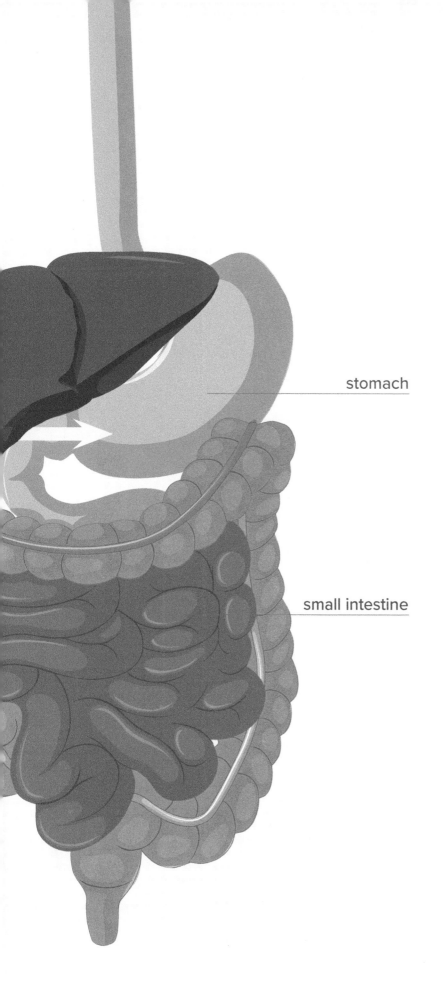

stomach

small intestine

Your liver is a large organ just next to your stomach on the right-hand side of your body. Its job is to finish getting your pizza ready to be carried along by your blood and used by your cells.

Your liver also sends a liquid called **bile** to your small intestine. This helps finish digesting the fats in your pizza—the cheese, the oils and the fatty parts of meat like pepperoni.

Once your liver has fully prepared your digested food, the liquids and microscopic pieces of food are picked up by your capillaries. They pass into your bloodstream and are carried to your hungry cells.

EXCRETORY SYSTEM

(EK skruh tor ee)

If you think about it, your blood circulates around and throughout your body over and over and over. To keep on doing its oxygen and food-carrying jobs, it has to be constantly cleaned. This cleaning is done by your **excretory system**. **Excrete** (ik SKREET) means getting rid of a body's waste products, and that's what this system does.

Some of the waste products from cells are harmful to your body, so your liver protects you by cleaning your blood. It filters out these harmful waste products and sends them to your **large intestine**, the last part of your digestive system where solid waste is prepared to leave your body.

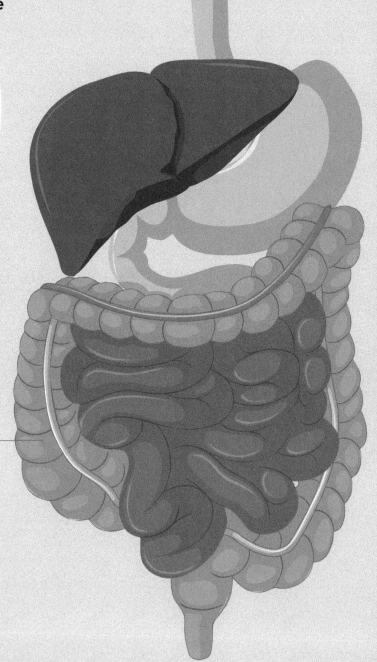

large intestine

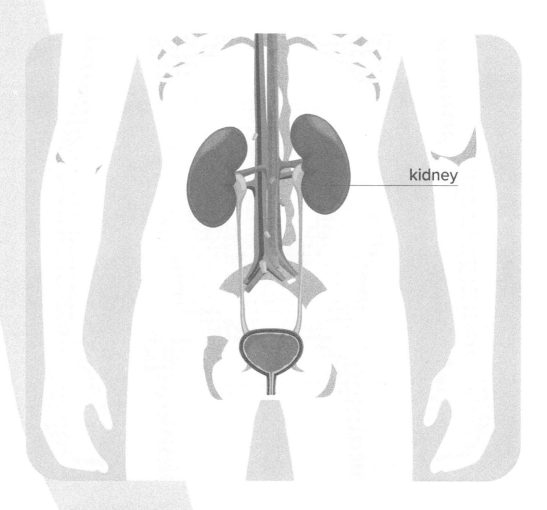

kidney

Your **kidneys** also clean your blood. This pair of bean-shaped organs sits on either side of your spine, in your lower back. As your blood passes through your kidneys, millions of tiny filters remove waste and your body gets rid of it as the liquid waste called urine.

Here is a simple picture to make it easy to see how blood circulates between all these systems.

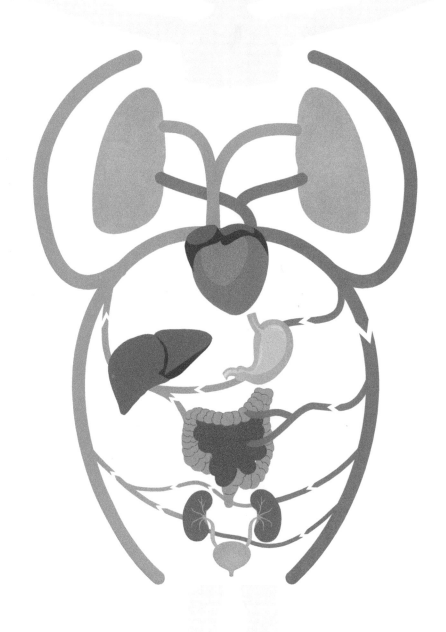

FIND THE PARTS!

Let's Do This!

For this activity you will need

- plastic heart model

Steps

1 Using your model heart and the illustrations on page 50, practice finding these parts of the body.

- ○ right upper chamber (heart)
- ○ right lower chamber (heart)
- ○ left upper chamber (heart)
- ○ left lower chamber (heart)
- ○ upper vena cava
- ○ lower vena cava
- ○ aorta
- ○ two arteries to upper body and arms
- ○ two arteries to head
- ○ two veins from head
- ○ lungs
- ○ right pulmonary artery
- ○ left pulmonary artery
- ○ right pulmonary veins

- ○ left pulmonary veins
- ○ liver
- ○ stomach
- ○ small intestine
- ○ large intestine
- ○ vein from small intestine to liver
- ○ artery from aorta to liver
- ○ vein from liver to lower vena cava
- ○ artery from aorta to small intestine
- ○ kidneys
- ○ arteries from aorta to kidneys
- ○ veins from kidneys to lower vena cava

2 When you are ready, have another person who is familiar with the information ask you to point out all the parts. Finish the activity when you can point out every part asked for without having to think about it.

PUTTING IT ALL TOGETHER

6

Your circulatory system has some great partners that help it do its job.

Your respiratory system gives it oxygen and carries carbon dioxide away.

Your digestive system turns what you eat into something your blood can carry to your cells to feed them.

And your excretory system helps clean your blood and get rid of wastes.

These systems work together, minute after minute, hour after hour, day after day. Your heart keeps on pumping, your blood circulates, your cells are fed and wastes are filtered out and carried away.

Around and around and around goes your blood! Never stopping, always flowing, keeping your body just as you like it, healthy and ready to go!

What other remarkable stories are
there to learn about your body?

You're a young scientist.
Go find out!

PUT IT ALL TOGETHER

For this activity you will need

- a piece of drawing paper as tall as you are and at least 30 inches wide.

- colored pencils or markers

- buttons or small squares of paper

Steps

1. Lie on the drawing paper and have another person make an outline of your body.

2. Use the body outline to make a drawing of the circulatory system and other body systems from the list in the last activity. Your drawing should look something like the picture on page 50. (You don't need to draw the body systems on top of each other.)

3. Color the veins and arteries and label the heart, lungs, liver, stomach, intestines, kidneys and major veins and arteries.

4. Using buttons or small squares of paper to represent rbcs, oxygen, carbon dioxide, cell food and cell wastes, show another person the path of blood from the heart to the lungs to the body and back to the heart. Show all the main paths the blood can take as it circulates through the body and tell what it does at each stop. (Remember that the rbcs carry oxygen and carbon dioxide, but blood plasma carries rbcs, cell food and other cell wastes.)

Printed in the USA
CPSIA information can be obtained
at www.ICGtesting.com
JSHW042049260324
59920JS00014B/59

THE FABULOUS HUMAN BODY

ANATOMY
for Young Scientists

THE FABULOUS HUMAN BODY

ANATOMY
for Young Scientists

Published by
Heron Books, Inc.
20950 SW Rock Creek Road
Sheridan, OR 97378

heronbooks.com

Special thanks to all the teachers and students who
provided feedback instrumental to this edition.

ISBN: 978-0-89-739239-6

Printed in the USA

13 May 2021

At Heron Books, we think learning should be engaging and fun. It should be hands-on and allow students to move at their own pace.

To facilitate this we have created a learning guide that will help any student progress through this book, chapter by chapter, with confidence and interest.

Get learning guides at
heronbooks.com/learningguides.

For teacher resources,
such as a final exam, email
teacherresources@heronbooks.com.

We would love to hear from you!
Email us at *feedback@heronbooks.com.*

Your
YOUNG SCIENTIST JOURNAL

Scientists love to explore the world and how things in it work. They like to go new places and discover things they've never seen before.

They also like to keep track of what they find. They often fill books with notes and drawings of what they see, and include their thoughts and questions about it. These books are called *science journals.*

What's fun about a science journal is that you can use it to draw pictures or sketches of things that interest you. You can write down ideas you have about things, make maps, write down questions you have and things you want to find out more about. You might even stick in it samples of things you find—flowers, bugs, leaves, feathers, spider's webs—who knows what?

Young Scientist
JOURNAL

The learning guide that goes with this book will sometimes ask you to look at things and make notes or drawings in a journal of your own.

Whatever you put in your science journal, it will be full of your own personal discoveries. No two journals are alike.

You can use a journal like the one shown here, or you can use a notebook of your choice. You might even want to make your own science journal and use that.

Whichever type of journal you choose, it will be a place to keep drawings and notes about what you are finding out about the world and how it works.

So get ahold of a science journal, or make one, and then get going to see what you can find out. Who knows what might be waiting for you?

IN THIS BOOK

YOUR FABULOUS MACHINE

If you think about it, the human body is a kind of machine. You use it to move around and do all the things you want to do. It is a machine that is fascinating and full of surprises!

Scientists have been studying the human body for centuries and are still discovering new things about it all the time.

How does the heart work exactly?

What happens when you breathe?

What does your stomach do?

And what about your muscles and bones? How do they work and what do they do exactly?

Well, answers to these questions and more are what this book is all about. It's about the subject of **human anatomy** (uh NAT uh mee). Anatomy tells us what the parts of the body are, and how they fit together.

So, how does this fabulous machine called the human body work? Let's take a look!

TRILLIONS OF LIVING THINGS

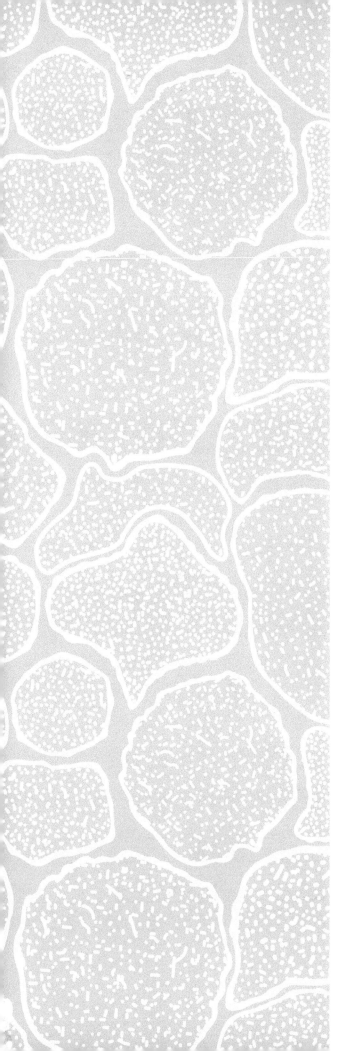

THE SMALLEST PART

The world is full of living things. There are trees, cats, grass, giraffes, bees and birds. There are spiders and flies, flowers and mushrooms, fish and even algae, the green stuff that grows on the water of a pond.

The smallest living part of each and every one of these is something called a **cell**. Your whole body, every large and small part, is made of cells.

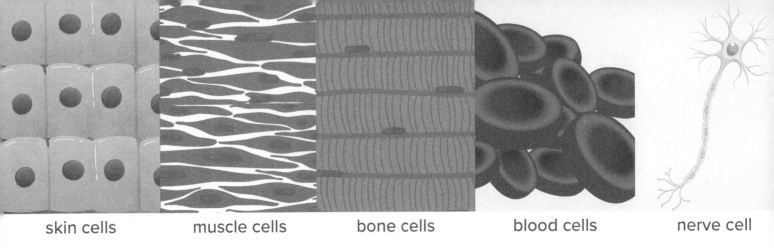

skin cells   muscle cells   bone cells   blood cells   nerve cell

If you look at your hand right now, you are looking at a bunch of skin cells. But you can't actually see the individual cells because they are so small you can only see them with a microscope.

Every human body is made up of millions and millions of cells. In fact, scientists think each person's body is made up of 30 trillion cells. That's 30,000,000,000,000!

And there are many different kinds of cells. There are muscle cells, bone cells, blood cells, nerve cells and more.

CELLS ARE ALIVE

Even though cells are extremely small, they live and die just like larger living things. And like larger living things, cells need food and water.

The cells in your body get food and water from the foods you eat and the liquids you drink. Have you ever been really hungry? That's your cells saying, "We need food!"

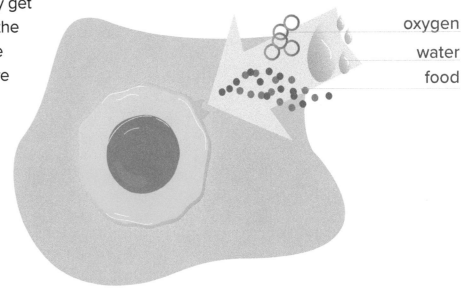

oxygen

water

food

Another thing that cells need is oxygen from the air. That's why you breathe.

Your cells use food, water and oxygen as fuel to keep you warm, and to help you move around and do things.

A cell grows, and then it divides into two cells. This makes another, new cell of the same kind. This is the way you get more cells, and this is how your body grows.

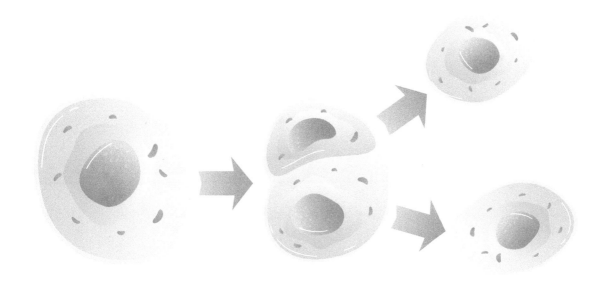

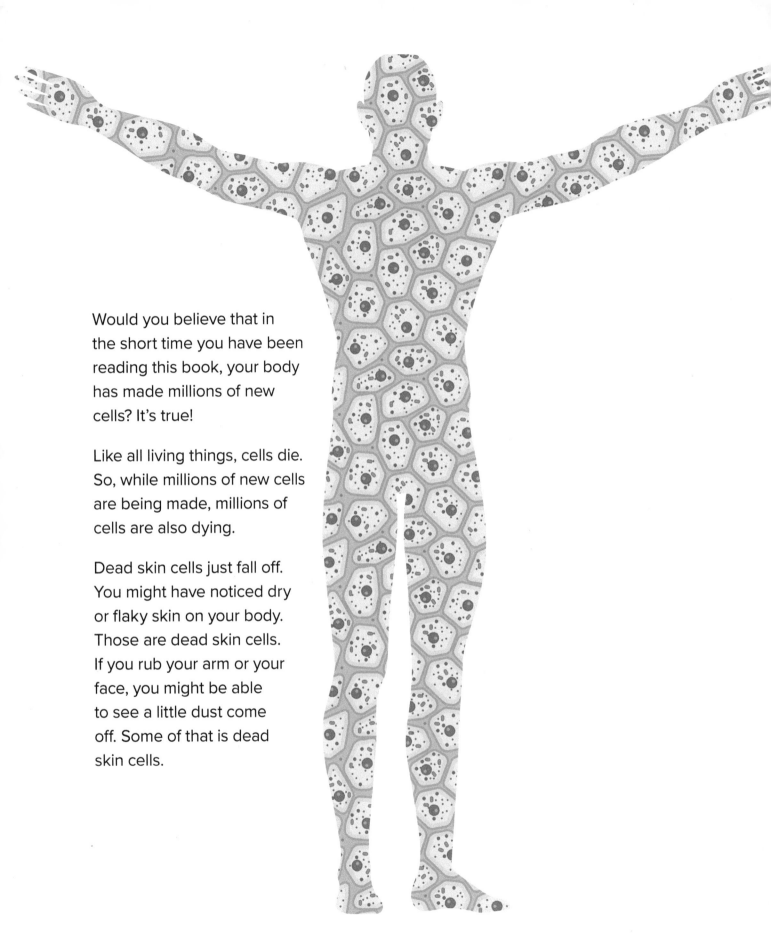

Would you believe that in the short time you have been reading this book, your body has made millions of new cells? It's true!

Like all living things, cells die. So, while millions of new cells are being made, millions of cells are also dying.

Dead skin cells just fall off. You might have noticed dry or flaky skin on your body. Those are dead skin cells. If you rub your arm or your face, you might be able to see a little dust come off. Some of that is dead skin cells.

CELLS GET RID OF WASTE

After cells use food, water and oxygen, there are always some things left over. These are called **wastes**.

Some liquid wastes become urine, which is the yellow liquid your body gets rid of when you go to the bathroom. Other liquid wastes come out of your skin as sweat.

What about the air you breathe out? That is cell waste, too. When cells use oxygen, this produces a waste called **carbon dioxide** (KAR bun dye AHK side).

Your cells also give off heat, which helps keep you warm.

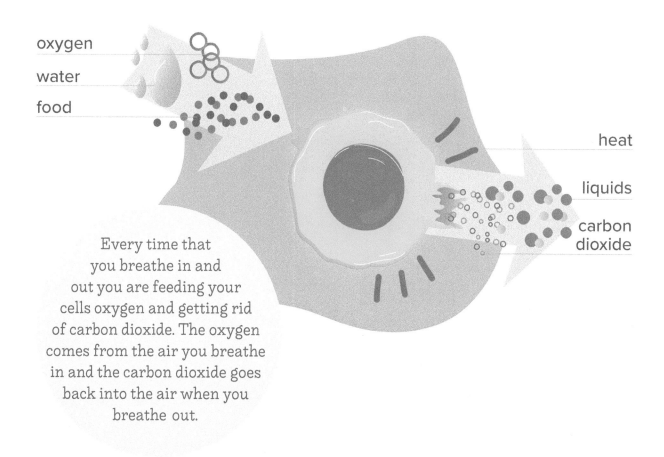

oxygen

water

food

heat

liquids

carbon dioxide

Every time that you breathe in and out you are feeding your cells oxygen and getting rid of carbon dioxide. The oxygen comes from the air you breathe in and the carbon dioxide goes back into the air when you breathe out.

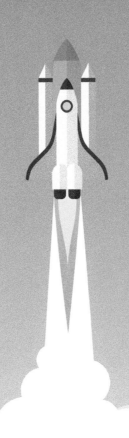

LITTLE MACHINE, BIG MACHINE

This book is all about the fabulous machine, your body.

Let's talk some more about why we call it a machine.

A **machine** is something you use to do work. Often that means you use it to help you move things.

Machines like rockets and motorcycles run by burning some kind of **fuel**. This gives them energy. Gasoline is an example of a fuel used to make cars, trucks, motorcycles and boats run.

Your body works the same way. You give it fuel and it uses the fuel to move your legs and arms, your eyes and mouth, and other body parts. Of course, you don't use gasoline to run your body. You use food, water and oxygen for fuel, and this makes it possible for you to move around.

Machines, like rockets and motorcycles, also produce heat and waste products like smoke. Have you ever seen a rocket launch? The fuel burns fast and out of the rocket flies smoke and a lot of heat!

Your body works the same way.

It takes in fuel and uses it for motion and heat. Your body doesn't smoke like a

launching rocket, but it does make waste. In addition to getting rid of carbon dioxide and sweat, you use the toilet several times a day to get rid of the body's liquid and solid wastes.

Your body has millions and millions of these little machines called cells.

They all work together to run the fabulous big machine, your body!

BUILDING BLOCKS OF LIFE

Now we know that cells are the smallest part of every living thing.

Your body has many different kinds of cells, but they all have certain things in common.

They are alive.

They are little machines that take in fuel and put out heat and waste.

They live, they grow and they die.

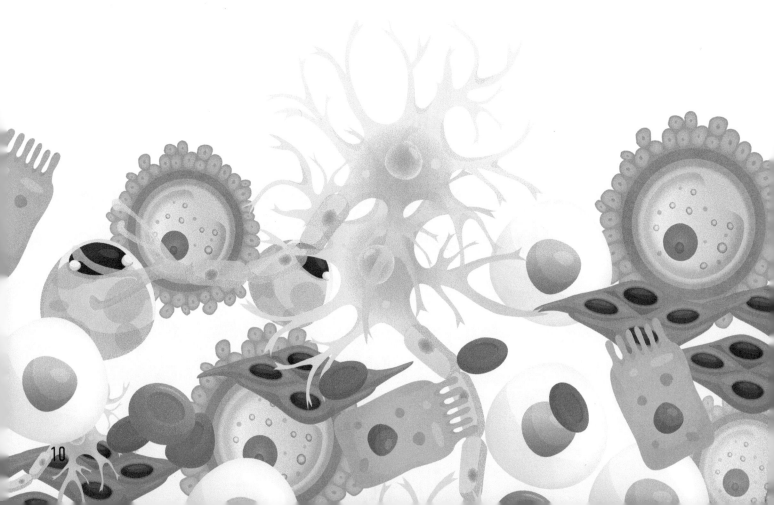

Cells are actually quite magical. They are often called "the building blocks of life."

Think about it. Without cells, there would be no living things on Earth!

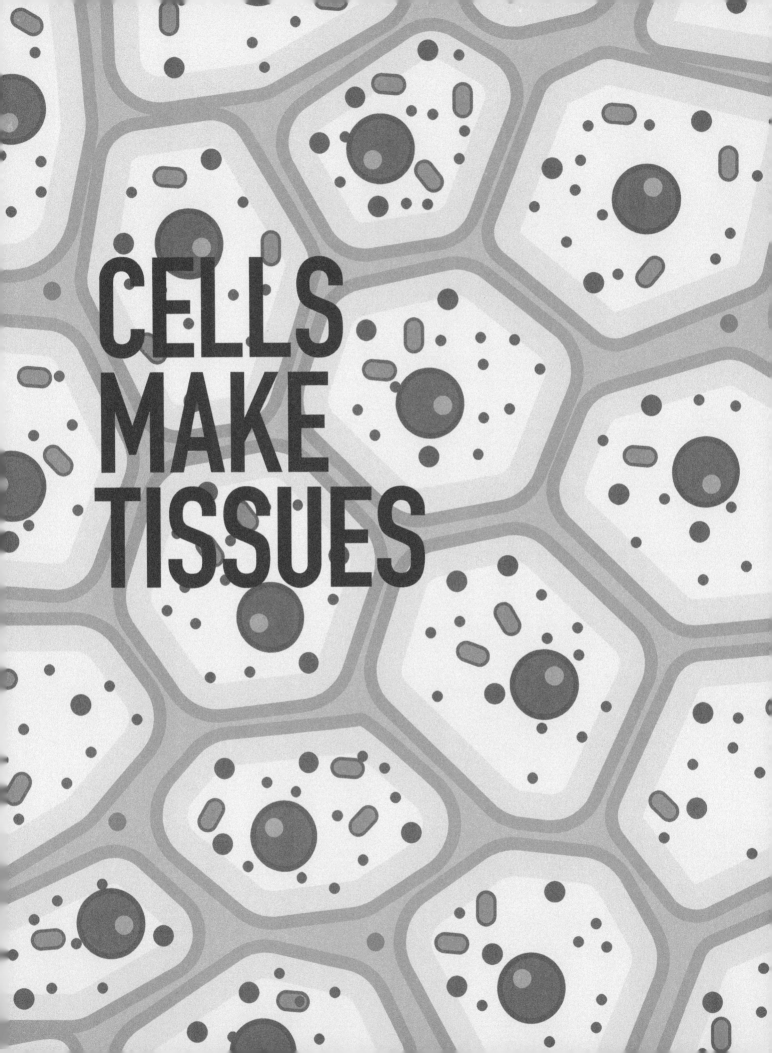

CELLS
MAKE
TISSUES

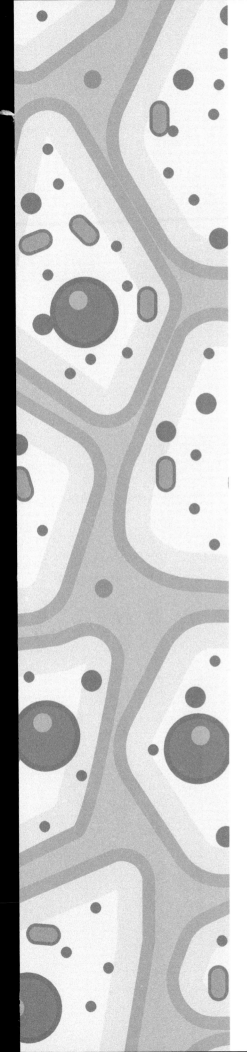

3

Every single cell in your body has a job
to do. Cells that have the same job work
together in groups to get that job done.
When cells of the same kind live and work
together, we call that group a **tissue** (TISH oo).

Muscle tissue is a group of muscle cells working together to make some part of your body move.

Muscle tissue looks like this:

Fat cells that live and work together are called fat tissue. It looks like this:

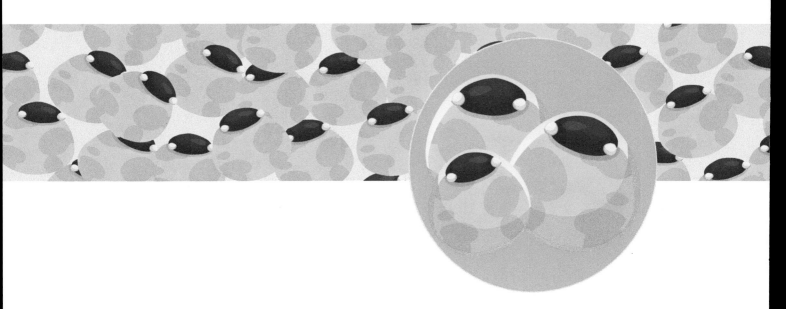

As you know, when you take in food, that food gets used for heat and movement. But if you take in energy that your body doesn't need right away, it stores up that energy in your fat tissue. The fat tissue holds on to it until you need it. Fat tissue also helps keep your body warm by providing a layer between your skin and the valuable insides of your body, like your heart and stomach.

Bone cells combine to make bone tissue. This gives your body a shape and makes it possible for you to move around. If you were just a shapeless blob, how would you ever get anywhere?

Brain cells make brain tissue. It directs all the parts of your body and helps them work together.

Within the fabulous human body, there are lots of different kinds of cells working together to make many different kinds of tissue.

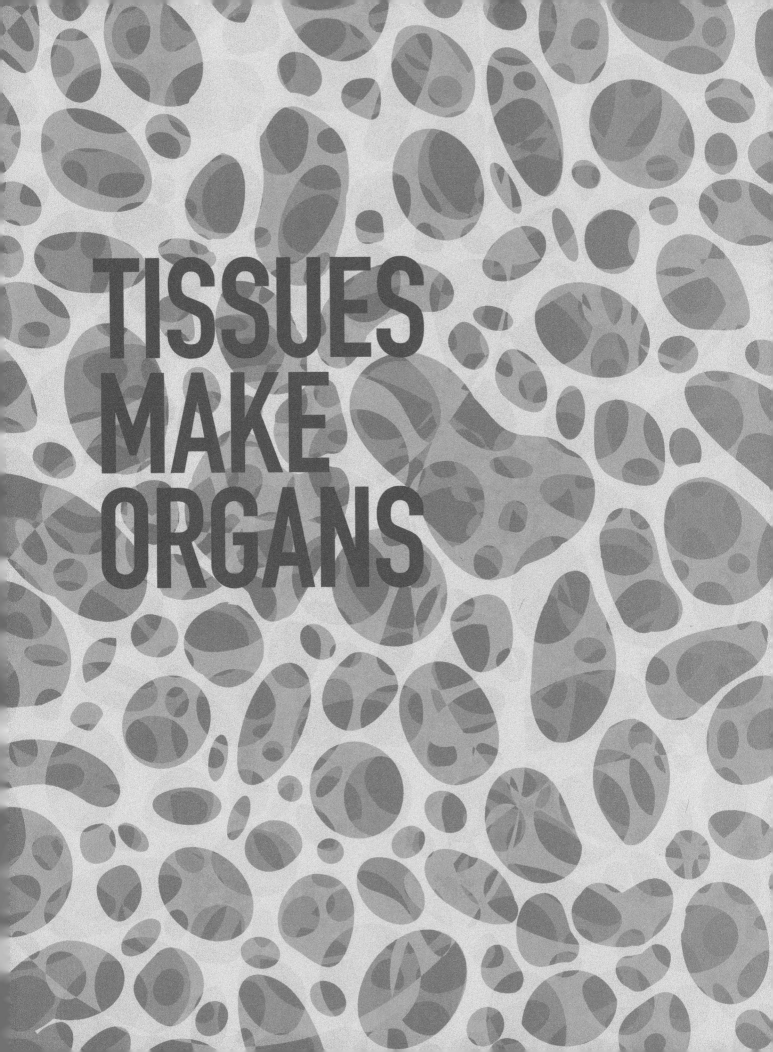

TISSUES
MAKE
ORGANS

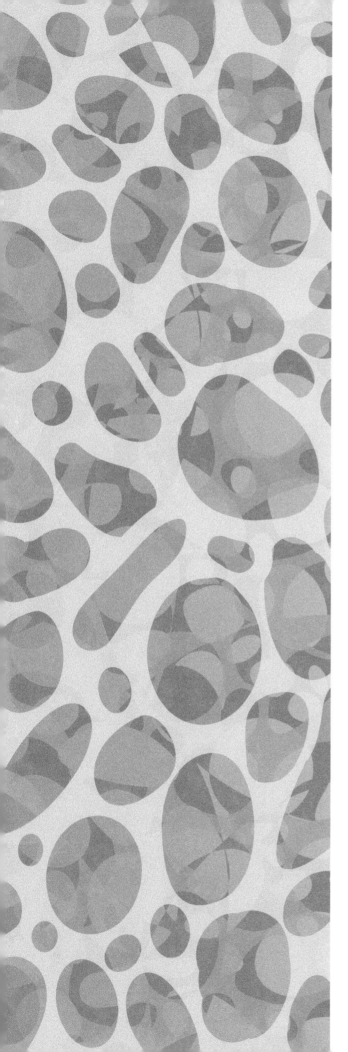

4

As you've seen, different kinds of tissues team up to get important jobs in the body done.

Tissues that are teamed up this way form organs. An **organ** (OR gun) is a part of the body that does a very specific job.

Your heart, for example, is an organ that sends blood to all the different parts of your body.

Your stomach is an organ that helps make the food you eat into something your cells can use as fuel.

Your lungs are organs that help you take in oxygen and get it into your blood so cells can use it.

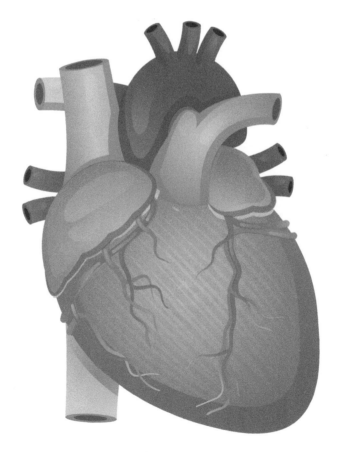

heart

Even your tongue is an organ. It has muscle tissue for moving food around in your mouth and for helping you make different sounds when you talk. It also has tissue made up of special cells that help you taste things.

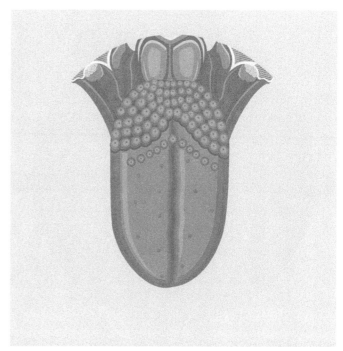

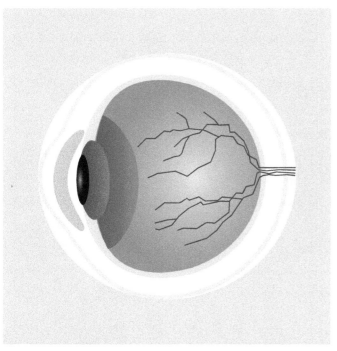

Your eyes are organs. They have muscle tissue that allows you to look in different directions, and tissue that senses light and lets you see.

There are many organs doing all the jobs necessary to keep your body working well.

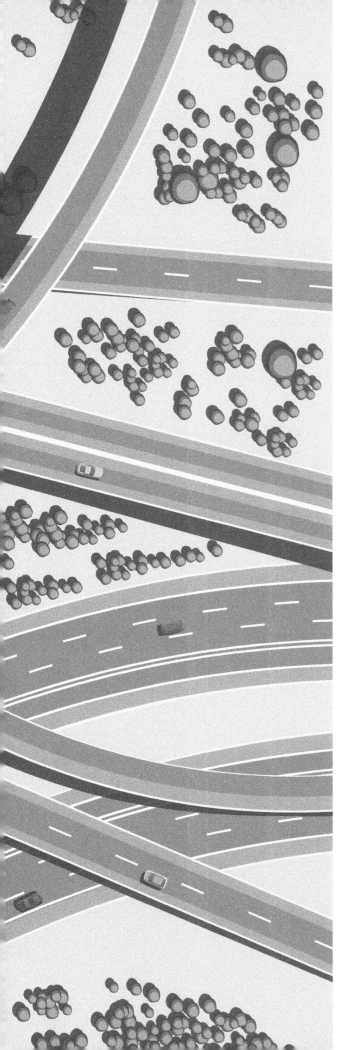

5

A **system** is a group of things working together.

Your house or apartment building probably has some kind of heating system. This would be all the parts that work together to heat the rooms.

Most countries have a system of highways that connect and work together to allow people to travel to all the different parts of the country.

A computer screen, speakers, mouse, keyboard, and the wires that connect them all together make a computer system.

Your body has different systems as well. There is a system that digests your food, a system that moves your blood around, and a system for sending messages to and from the brain.

When certain organs work closely together, they form a system.

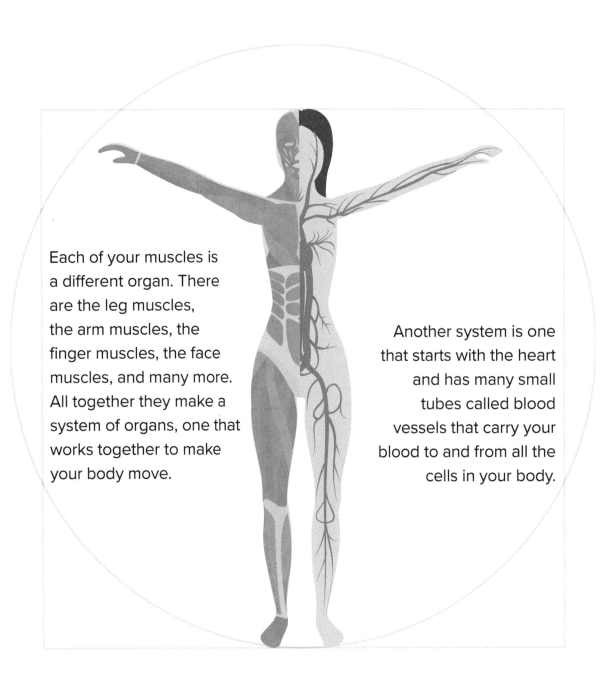

Each of your muscles is a different organ. There are the leg muscles, the arm muscles, the finger muscles, the face muscles, and many more. All together they make a system of organs, one that works together to make your body move.

Another system is one that starts with the heart and has many small tubes called blood vessels that carry your blood to and from all the cells in your body.

But before we move on to talk about all these amazing systems, let's take a moment to look again at how the body is put together:

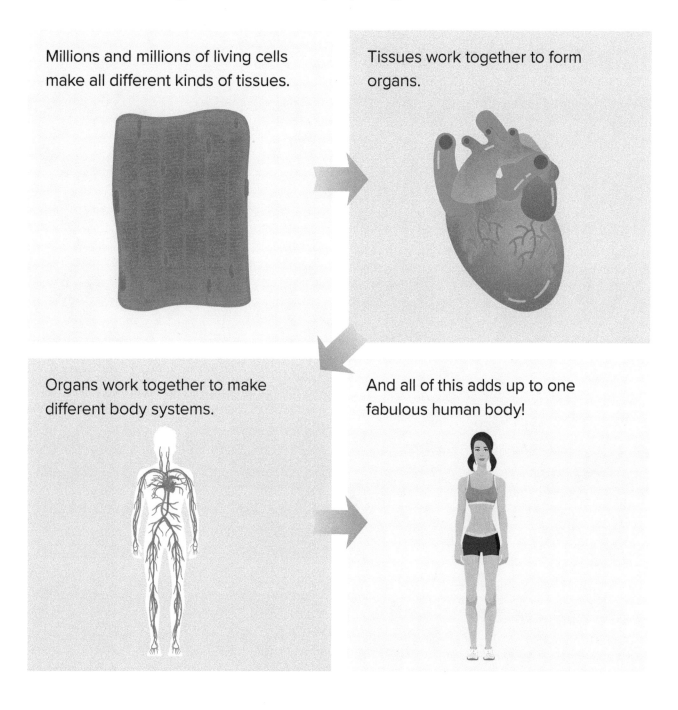

Millions and millions of living cells make all different kinds of tissues.

Tissues work together to form organs.

Organs work together to make different body systems.

And all of this adds up to one fabulous human body!

Human anatomy really is quite amazing. You might be starting to see why scientists keep studying it to learn more and more about it.

So, are you ready to take a closer look at some of the most important systems in the body?

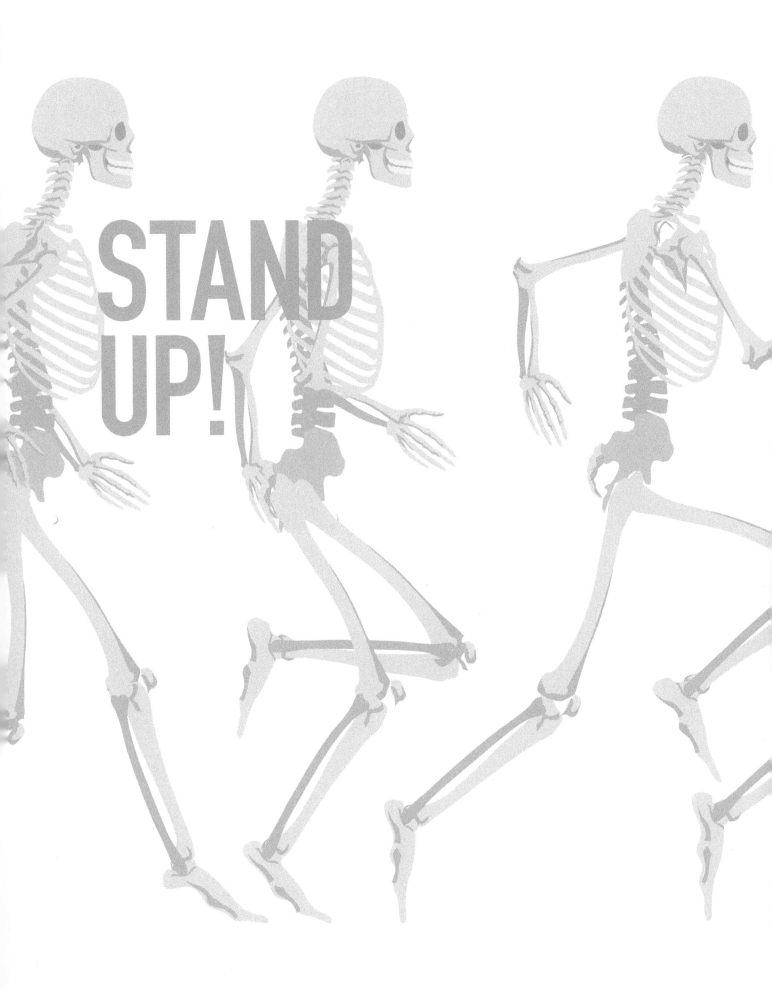

STAND
UP!

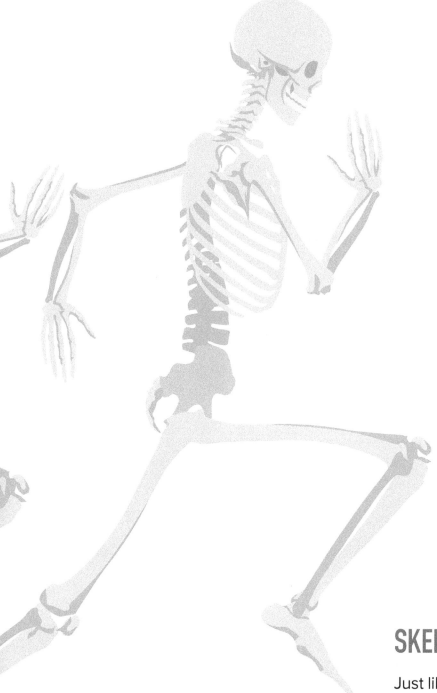

6

The human
body has about
210 individual bones!
Even though that may
seem like a lot, the
number of bones in a
cat is 230!

SKELETON

Just like your muscles or your heart,
bones are made of different tissues
that work together. Every bone is an
organ. All the bones together make up
the **skeleton**.

All of your bones work together to make a system called the **skeletal** (SKEL uh tul) **system**. The jobs of the skeletal system are these:

- hold your body's shape

- protect important organs inside your body

- give muscles something to attach to, so you can move

- make your blood cells (yes, bones make blood cells!)

The protection job that bones do is an important one. If you didn't have ribs, a punch to the chest could easily damage your heart or lungs. Or a bump on the head could hurt your brain if you didn't have thick bone surrounding it.

Holding the body's shape is another important job done by the skeletal system. Without bones, you wouldn't be able to stand up!

JOINTS

The place where two or more bones come together in a way that lets them move is called a **joint**. Your knee, for example, is a joint. It joins the bone in your upper leg to the bone in your lower leg in a way that lets your leg bend.

Many joints work like the hinges on a door. They connect bones together in a way that allows them to move.

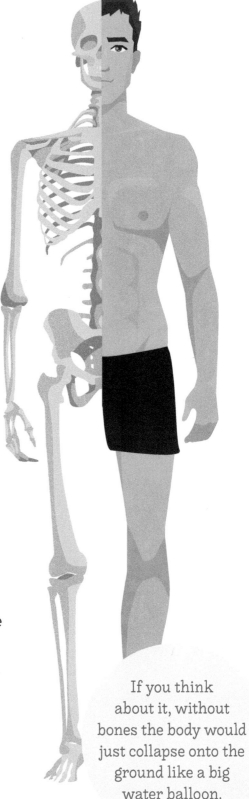

If you think about it, without bones the body would just collapse onto the ground like a big water balloon.

If you take a minute to move your body around, you will probably notice you have lots of joints. Without them you would not be able to move many different parts of your body!

The bones of your hands not only hold the hand and fingers together but their joints allow you to move your hands and fingers in many useful ways.

elbow joint

wrist joint

finger joints

Like your hands, your feet have many joints. These allow your foot to move so you can walk, run, jump, dance or just wiggle your toes.

Your **elbow** is a joint where the bone of your upper arm connects to the bones of your lower arm. It allows your lower arm to move toward or away from your upper arm.

The bones of your feet hold your feet and toes in the right position.

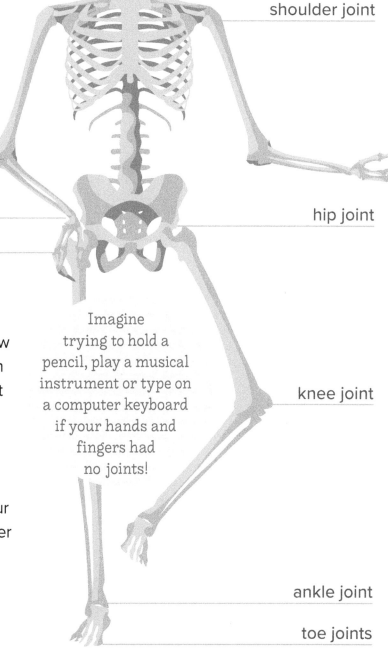

neck joints

shoulder joint

hip joint

Imagine trying to hold a pencil, play a musical instrument or type on a computer keyboard if your hands and fingers had no joints!

knee joint

ankle joint

toe joints

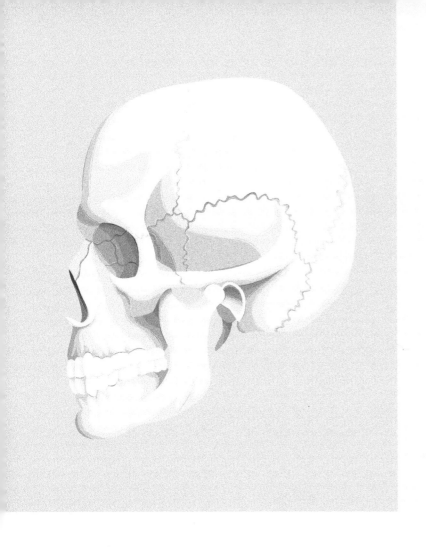

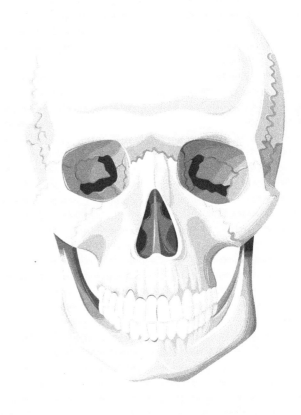

SKULL AND TEETH

Your **skull** is a collection of 22 bones that form the shape of your head and protect your brain inside. At birth, a human's skull is softer. It can take a year or more for the parts of a baby's skull to finish growing together into its stronger shape.

What about your teeth? Teeth aren't living organs like bones, but because they are so much like bones, we think of them as part of the skeletal system. Your **teeth** are used to bite food into pieces and to chew it up so you can swallow it.

There is only one part of the skull that moves. It's the jawbone. Imagine what would happen if you couldn't move your jaw!

SPINE AND RIBS

Your **spine**, or backbone, holds your body upright. It allows you to bend forward, backward, and side to side. It also protects special tissues that send messages to and from your brain.

Your **rib cage** is made of bones that look like a cage around your chest. It has 12 rib bones on each side, and these are attached to your spine.

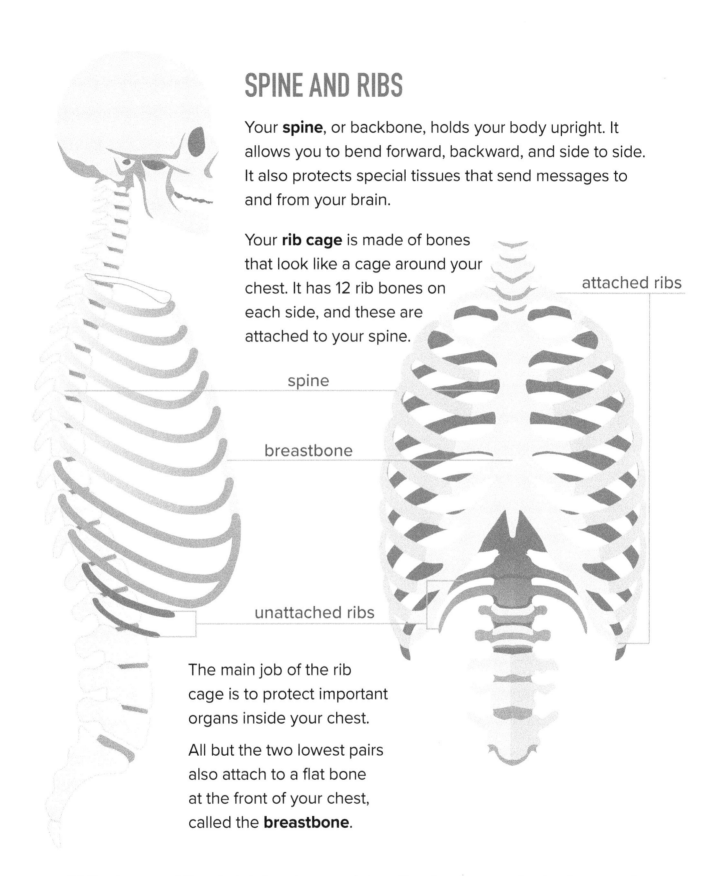

attached ribs

spine

breastbone

unattached ribs

The main job of the rib cage is to protect important organs inside your chest.

All but the two lowest pairs also attach to a flat bone at the front of your chest, called the **breastbone**.

All the bones of the skeletal system work together to give your body shape and to protect the soft tissues and organs inside.

MOVE!

7

MUSCLES

How do you run, jump, skip, dance and move your body in other ways? You do it with your muscles, of course.

All the muscles together are called the **muscular** (MUS kyuh lur) **system**.

You use your muscular system to lift things, move things, smile, blink, and talk. You even use a muscle under your lungs to pull air in and push it out.

The human muscular system has 639 muscles throughout the entire body.

But if you think that's a lot, you might be interested in knowing that an elephant's trunk all by itself has over 40,000 muscles!

HOW MUSCLES WORK

The way muscles work is by flexing and relaxing. **Flexing** a muscle means making it shorter and tighter. When you flex a muscle, you make it bunch up into a tighter, harder shape.

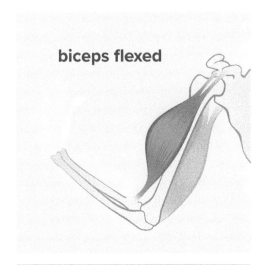

biceps flexed

Pull your hand up and touch your shoulder. Can you feel the flexed muscle in your upper arm? Now relax the muscle and let your hand drop back down.

The muscle in your upper arm that pulls your lower arm up toward your shoulder is called your **biceps** (BY seps).

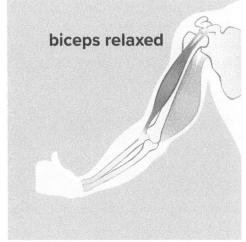

biceps relaxed

Now try smiling. Can you feel the muscles in your face flex as they get tighter and harder and pull your mouth into a curve? If you relax your face muscles, your smile goes away and those muscles feel like they aren't flexed anymore.

Now let's go back to your arm. The muscle underneath your upper arm that pushes your lower arm away from your shoulder is called your **triceps** (TRY seps). When you bend your elbow and bring your hand to your shoulder, your biceps is flexed and your triceps is relaxed.

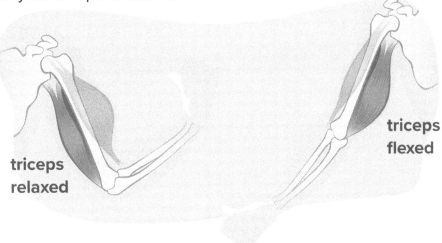

triceps relaxed

triceps flexed

When you stretch your arm out straight, your triceps is flexed, and your biceps is relaxed.

Your **calf muscle** is on the back of your leg below your knee. You use your calf muscle to jump into the air or push your body forward when walking or running. Strong calf muscles help you jump high and run fast.

When you make your muscles work hard, some of the cells and tissues break down a little bit. Have you ever felt muscles being tired or sore? That's a sign they have broken down some. The good news is that as they heal, they try to build back up even stronger.

Now you know one way to build strong muscles. Use them a lot and they will get stronger over time.

CONNECTING TO BONES

A **tendon** (TEN duhn) is a special kind of tissue that connects a muscle to a bone, or to some other part of the body. Tendons are strong and flexible like muscles, but they don't stretch as much.

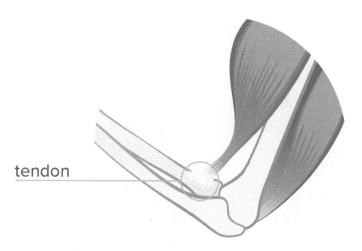

tendon

Your **Achilles** (uh KIL eez) **tendon**, for example, connects your calf muscle to the bone in your heel. This way you can use your calf muscle to move your foot and ankle so you can run, walk and jump.

Achilles tendon

The Achilles tendon is named after a warrior in a very old story. The warrior's name was Achilles. When he was a baby, his goddess mother held him by his heel and dipped him into a magic river that was supposed to make him god-like, not human, so he couldn't be killed. But she forgot to let the water touch the heel where she was holding him. This meant he could still be hurt there. Achilles grew up to be a great warrior, but he was killed by an arrow that hit him right in that spot!

There are thousands of tendons throughout the body, including four in the shoulder and two in the knee. Tendons have an important job in the muscular system because they help your muscles move your bones. They help you run, jump, skip, dance and do many, many other things.

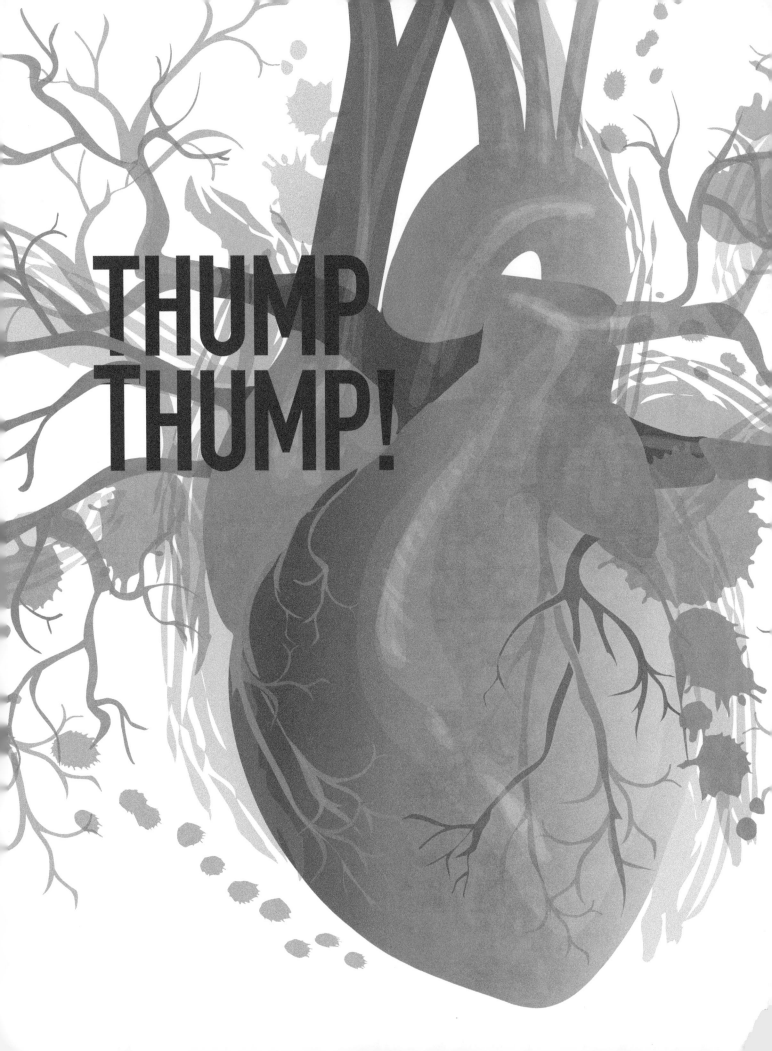

THUMP
THUMP!

8

Circulate (SUR kyuh late) means go around in a circular pattern. When something circulates, it starts in one place, moves around and ends up back where it started.

That's what your blood does. Starting from your heart, it moves around the body, and comes back to your heart to get pushed around again and again. The name of this system is the **circulatory** (SUR kyuh luh tor ee) **system**.

Your circulatory system carries blood to and from all parts of your body. Your blood is like a river that carries food and oxygen to your cells and then picks up cell waste and carries it away. In the middle of it all is the heart.

Your **heart** is a pump that keeps your blood flowing. It pumps your blood through your blood vessels to all parts of your body and back again. Your heart is a special kind of muscle, so you could say it is part of the muscular system. But its most important job is pumping blood, so we call it part of the circulatory system.

The heart sends blood filled with oxygen to all the cells in your body. While it's going around, your blood picks up waste like carbon dioxide from your cells.

Your heart and your lungs work closely together. Your lungs put fresh oxygen into your blood and send it to your heart for pumping to all your cells. Then your heart sends your blood with its carbon dioxide waste back to your lungs so you can get rid of it by breathing it out.

Imagine keeping trillions of cells supplied with oxygen! Fortunately, your heart has a whole system to help.

Put your hand on your chest. You may be able to feel your heart beating. If you can't, try pressing gently to the side of your throat or on the inside of your wrist on the thumb side. The thump thump you feel is called your **heartbeat**.

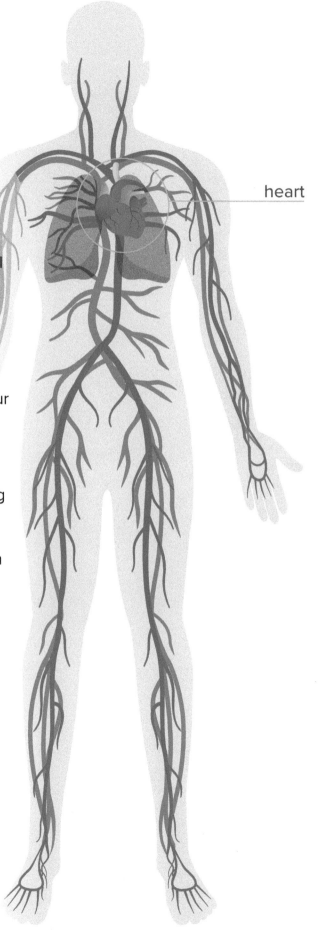

heart

A **blood vessel** (VES ul) is a tube that carries blood through your body. There are three types of blood vessels: arteries, veins and capillaries.

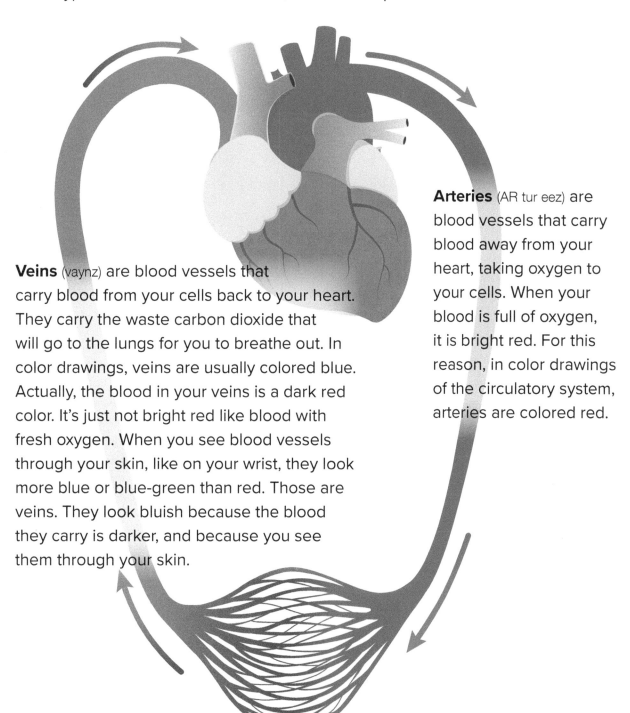

Veins (vaynz) are blood vessels that carry blood from your cells back to your heart. They carry the waste carbon dioxide that will go to the lungs for you to breathe out. In color drawings, veins are usually colored blue. Actually, the blood in your veins is a dark red color. It's just not bright red like blood with fresh oxygen. When you see blood vessels through your skin, like on your wrist, they look more blue or blue-green than red. Those are veins. They look bluish because the blood they carry is darker, and because you see them through your skin.

Arteries (AR tur eez) are blood vessels that carry blood away from your heart, taking oxygen to your cells. When your blood is full of oxygen, it is bright red. For this reason, in color drawings of the circulatory system, arteries are colored red.

The last group of blood vessels are called **capillaries** (KAP uh lair eez). These are tiny blood vessels that go to and from all the tiny cells in your body. How tiny are capillaries? They are 100 times thinner than a single hair on your head!

All these blood vessels and
the heart work together as
one big team.

Heart

The heart pumps the blood
around and around the body.

Veins

Your veins carry your blood,
full of carbon dioxide and
waste, back to your heart.

Capillaries

Capillaries carry blood from
your arteries into all the tiny
little places your cells live,
dropping off oxygen and food.
They pick up carbon dioxide
and other wastes and carry
them to your veins.

to lungs

from lungs

Your heart
pumps about
80 times each minute. If
you ran full speed for a bit,
it would pump even faster. If
you took a nap, it would slow
down. Why? Because how fast
or slow it beats depends on
how much oxygen your
cells need.

Arteries

Arteries carry blood that is full
of oxygen and food from the
heart to the cells.

Your blood is
made up of cells
too. How fast are those
blood cells moving around
your body? It normally takes
less than a minute for a blood
cell to leave your heart, reach
some part of your body
and get back to your
heart again!

Your blood really is going around and
around and around all the time, and
maybe faster than you realized.

BREATHE!

9

Let's talk more about the oxygen that all your cells need.

Humans are not special in their need for oxygen. All animals on Earth need oxygen to live. And when they use it for energy, it results in the waste product carbon dioxide.

What's interesting about life on Earth is that plants need oxygen too, but they don't get it from the air like most animals do. Plants take in carbon dioxide, that same thing we breathe out. Then they use sunlight to turn the carbon dioxide into oxygen they can use.

For human bodies, carbon dioxide is a waste. For plants it is not. The good thing for us is that plants give away more oxygen than they use. That means there's more oxygen for humans and other animals than there would be if we didn't have a planet full of plant life.

To get and use oxygen, a human body needs a system. This is where your respiratory (RES pruh tor ee) system comes in. **Respiratory** means having to do with breathing in and out. Your **respiratory system** lets you breathe in to get oxygen to your cells and breathe out to get rid of their carbon dioxide waste.

Windpipe

From your nose and mouth, air flows through a tube called your **windpipe**.

Lungs

Finally, the air arrives deep in your **lungs**, squishy bags of soft tissue that fill a large portion of your chest. So every time you take in a breath, air travels along a path that arrives in your lungs. And every time you breathe out, your lungs get rid of carbon dioxide along the same path.

Bronchi

The air moves from your windpipe into your lungs through two branch-like tubes called **bronchi** (BRONG kye). One by itself is called a **bronchus** (BRONG kus). One bronchus carries air to the left lung and the other carries it to the right lung.

Bronchioles

In your lungs the bronchi separate into thousands of tiny hair-like branches called **bronchioles** (BRONG kee ohlz).

You breathe in and out about 20 times every minute. If you are working your body hard, playing soccer, carrying something heavy, or dancing for example, you will notice yourself breathing many more times each minute.

The last part of your respiratory system is a large sheet of muscle that your lungs rest on. It's called the **diaphragm** (DYE uh fram).

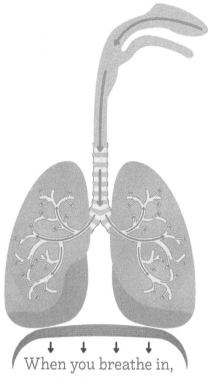

When you breathe in, your diaphragm moves downward. This leaves space and your lungs can fill up with fresh air.

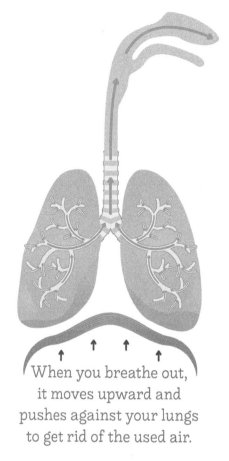

When you breathe out, it moves upward and pushes against your lungs to get rid of the used air.

Inside each lung are millions of tiny little sacs (bags of soft tissue) called **alveoli** (al VEE oh lye). Each time you breathe in, these tiny sacs fill with air. From these tiny sacs your capillaries pick up the oxygen you just breathed in and add it into the blood that's passing by. We know what happens then. It gets pumped around your body by your heart.

At the same time, the alveoli get carbon dioxide waste from the capillaries. When you breathe out, away goes the old air full of carbon dioxide. It goes out the way it came in—up through your bronchioles, bronchi and windpipe, and out your nose and mouth.

And all of this happens every few seconds, every minute, every hour, every day for your entire life!

10

Digestion (dye JES chun) is how your body breaks down food into much, much tinier parts so it can be used by your cells. Your **digestive** (dye JES tiv) **system** is made up of all the parts of your body that have to do with taking in food and turning it into something your cells can use. A number of your organs are part of your digestive system, and each one has its own special job.

Digestion starts in your mouth, where something interesting happens. Did you ever think about the fact that your body makes liquids?

When you are unhappy, your body makes tears that fill up around your eyes and run down your face. And when you see or smell something you really want to eat, what happens? Your mouth makes a liquid. That liquid is called **saliva**.

Saliva (suh LYE vuh) does an important job. It mixes with food in your mouth to soften it up, making it easier to chew and swallow. Chewing and saliva are the beginning of the digestive system because they start breaking a bite of food into small pieces.

Tears, sweat, saliva and other liquids are made by special, small organs called **glands**. You have tear glands above each eye and sweat glands in your skin. Glands for saliva are under your tongue and under and behind each jaw. **Salivary** (SAL uh vair ee) **glands** put saliva into your mouth through small tubes.

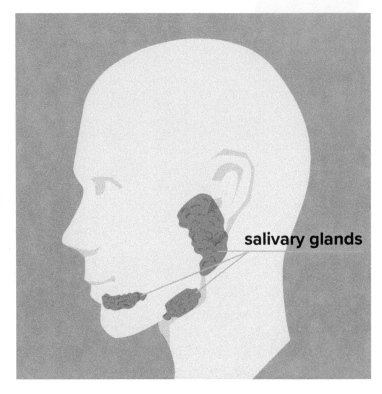

salivary glands

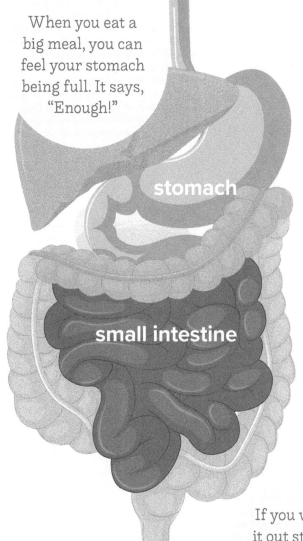

esophagus

stomach

small intestine

When you swallow, muscles in the back of your mouth and throat push the food back and down into a tube right behind your windpipe. This tube is called the **esophagus** (uh SOF uh guhs). It carries the food you eat from your mouth to your stomach.

Your **stomach** has an important job in digestion. It adds new liquids that help dissolve the chewed-up food. This results in a soupy liquid that is ready to move to the next organ.

This soupy liquid goes into a long tube that winds around like a folded-up hose. This long, winding tube is called the **small intestine** (in TES tin).

Once it's in the small intestine, this soupy liquid from your stomach is slowly broken down into tiny, tiny pieces small enough to be carried by your blood to all your hungry cells. How do these pieces get into your blood? Again, it's the capillaries doing their work. They pick up the food and put it into the circulatory system to be pumped around your body.

When you eat a big meal, you can feel your stomach being full. It says, "Enough!"

If you were to lay it out straight, the small intestine would be about 20 feet long. That's about as tall as a giraffe!

It takes about 6 to 8 hours for food to pass through your stomach and small intestine. But the intestine gets help from two more important organs that are part of the digestive system.

The first of these organs is called the **pancreas** (PANG kree us). It sits just behind and a little below your stomach.

The second one is the **liver** (LIV ur). This is a large organ that sits above your stomach on the right side.

Both of these organs have other jobs, but one job they both have is making certain liquids that help the small intestine break your food down so it can be used by your cells. These organs release their liquids into the small intestine and there it helps digest your food.

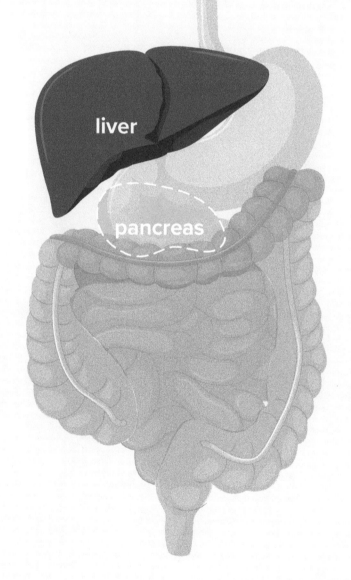

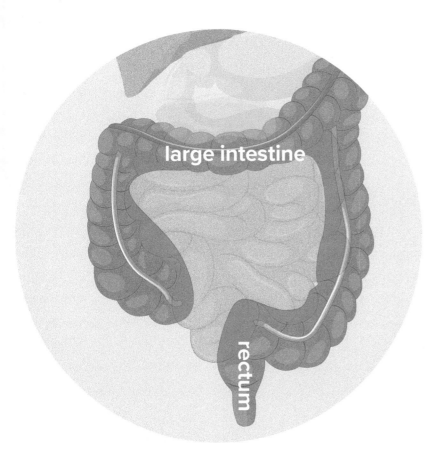

large intestine

rectum

Now that the food has been digested and sent to your cells, there are left-over bits and liquids that your body doesn't use. These pass along into another tube that curls around your small intestine. This is called the **large intestine**. Its job is to take most of the water out of the leftover part of your digested food, leaving the solid part behind. This solid material is called **feces** (FEE sees).

The waste materials we call feces get pushed out of your body by the very last organ in your digestive system. At the bottom end of your large intestine is the **rectum** (REK tum). The rectum stretches and this tells you it's time to go to the bathroom. The feces move from your large intestine and are passed out through your rectum.

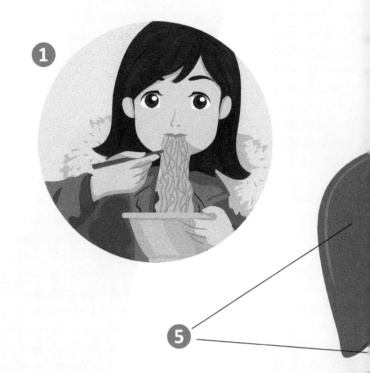

That's the end of each bite of food you've eaten. It has moved all the way

1 from your mouth,

2 through your esophagus,

3 to your stomach, where liquids were added to make it soupy,

4 to your small intestine,

5 where the liver and pancreas added other liquids, so the capillaries can take it to feed your cells,

6 to your large intestine,

7 and finally, out of your rectum, one, two or three days later!

The result of all this digestion? Millions and millions of happy, well-fed cells!

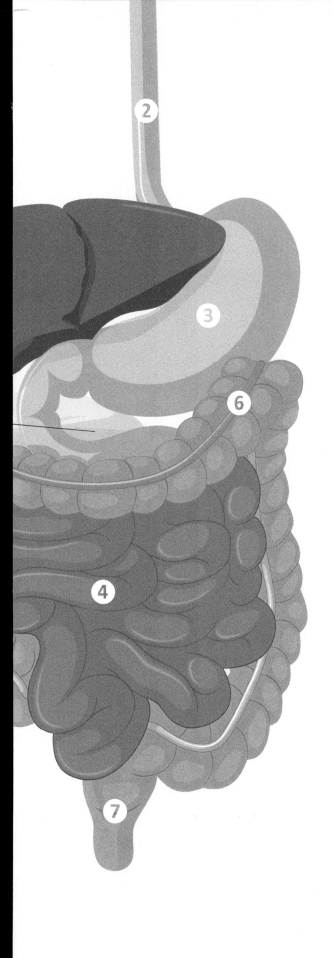

THIRSTY?

11

So, all those well-fed cells are happy, right? But suddenly you feel thirsty. Why is that? That's because your cells need more than oxygen and food. They need water too.

Did you know that over half of your body weight comes from water?

If you weigh 60 pounds, more than 30 pounds of that is water. That's about 4 gallons of water!

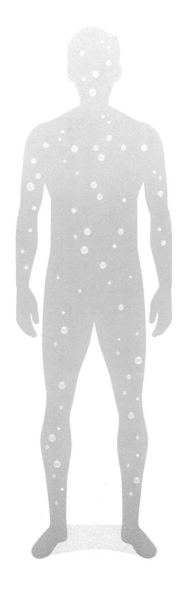

Where is all this water?

It's in your cells, your digestive system, your blood, and all your organs. It's even in your bones!

To give your cells water, you take in liquids every day. Some of it gets used and the body gets rid of the rest when you go to the bathroom.

What it gets rid of is called **urine** (YUR in). It's made of extra water and liquid wastes from the cells. The system that does this work is called the **urinary** (YUR uh nair ee) **system**.

Let's look at the main organs that make up this important system.

First, you have the **kidneys** (KID neez). This pair of organs is located inside your back, just under your ribcage on either side of the spine (backbone). Their job is to remove liquid wastes and extra water from your blood, making urine. They are blood cleaners.

The kidneys send the urine through tubes to a storage bag called the **bladder** (BLAD ur). When your bladder begins to fill up, you start to feel the need to go to the bathroom. When it's very full, you feel the need to go to the bathroom fast!

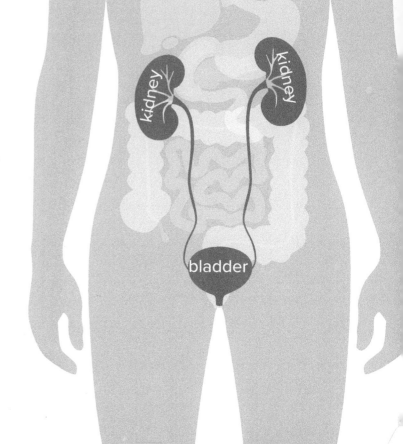

The amount of urine your body makes depends on many things, like how much you drink, how hard you are working or playing, and how hot or cold it is. If you are sweating a lot, your body is getting rid of some of its liquid wastes through the skin. This is not urine, it's sweat. The more you sweat, the less your bladder will fill up with liquid waste.

With enough oxygen, food and water, your cells can do their jobs. And the more you learn about the fabulous human body, the more you understand how many jobs all those cells have!

MOVING
MESSAGES

12

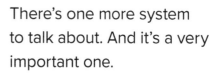

There's one more system to talk about. And it's a very important one.

Most people will say that the three most important organs in your body are your heart, your lungs and your brain. You know why your heart and lungs are important, so now let's talk about the brain and the system it belongs to.

This last system is all about nerves. **Nerves** are like threads running throughout your body. Their job is a little like electrical wires because they take messages from one part of your body to another very quickly.

Some nerve messages travel 300 feet per second. Imagine something moving from one soccer goal to the other in one second.

Look at your finger. Decide to move it, and then move it.

That was quick, wasn't it? That message was carried from your brain to your finger.

The name of this fast-moving system comes from the word "nerve." It is called the **nervous** (NUR vus) **system**. Normally, when you hear the word "nervous," it is describing a feeling like being worried and a little afraid. Here the word just means the system is all about the body's nerves.

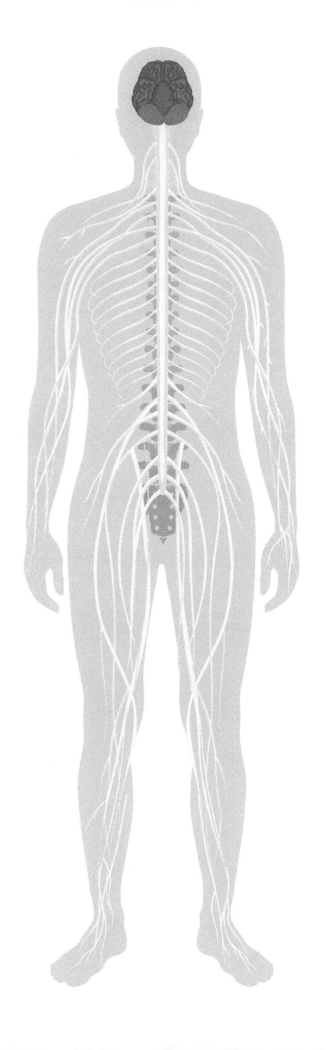

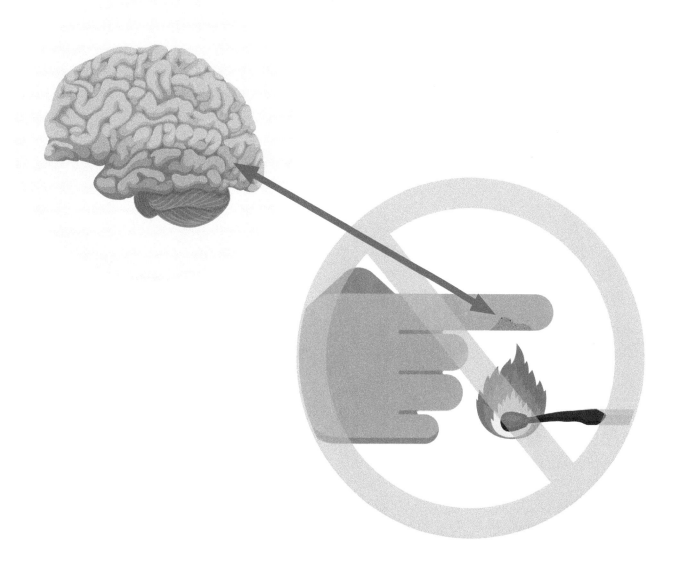

Your **brain** is the control center of your nervous system. Nerves carry messages between your brain and other parts of the body. For example, if you touch something hot, the message "hot!" goes to your brain and the message "stop touching!" comes back. Your muscles get the message, and your hand pulls away from the hot thing, probably so fast you don't even think about it.

Let's imagine you decide to run across a field. Your eyes see where you want to go, and your brain sends messages to your muscles that get your body running. As you run, you feel the air in your face, you see the ground moving under your feet, you hear the sound of your breath and you feel your feet brushing the grass. All these things you sense are sent as messages to your brain from your face, your eyes, your ears and your feet.

Messages are always going from parts of your body to your brain, and messages are always going from your brain to different parts of your body.

One part of your brain sends messages to organs like your heart, lungs and intestines that keep them working even when you aren't thinking about them. That's how your body keeps working even when you're asleep.

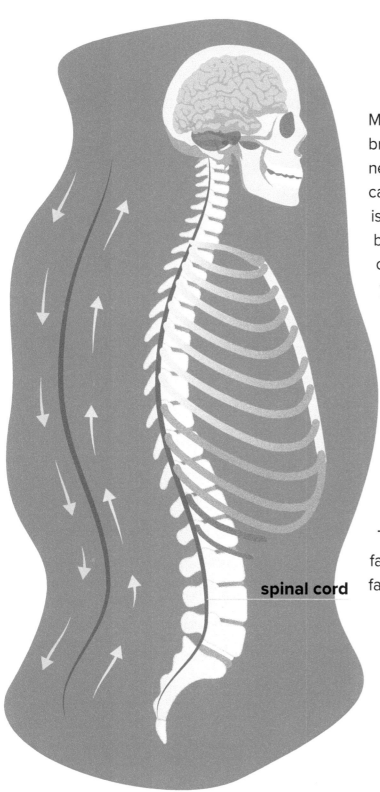

spinal cord

Messages travel to and from the brain through a large bundle of nerves running through your spine called the **spinal** (SPY nul) **cord.** This is the main pathway for messages between your brain and the rest of your body. The messages from your brain go through the spinal cord and out through hundreds of smaller and smaller nerves as they get further and further from the spine. Messages go back to the brain on this same path.

Imagine trying to run your body without the brain sending and receiving messages all the time.

The brain just might be the most fascinating organ in the amazing and fabulous human body!

A TRULY
AMAZING
MACHINE

13

By now, you probably agree that the human body, with all its different parts, is quite wonderful.

It is made of trillions and trillions of cells.

These cells make up different kinds of tissues.

Tissues work together to make all the different organs throughout your body.

Organs team up to form these important systems:

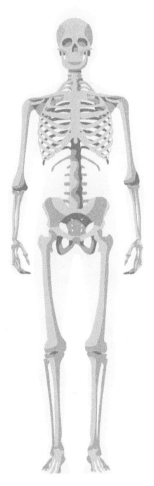

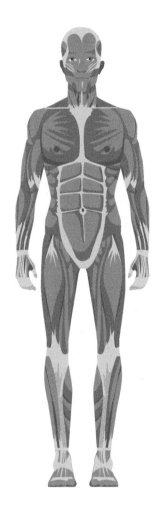

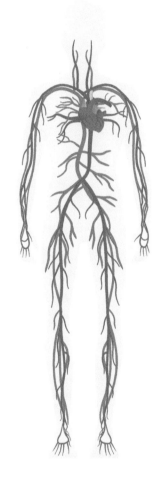

the **skeletal system**, which gives your body shape,

the **muscular system**, which allows your body to move,

the **circulatory system**, which moves blood all through your body,

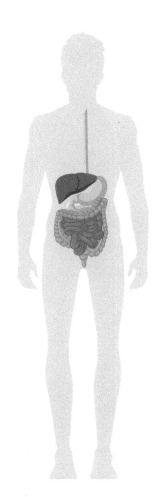

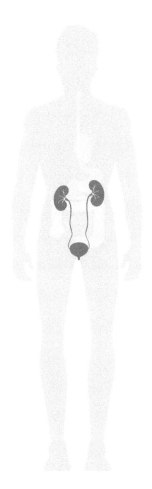

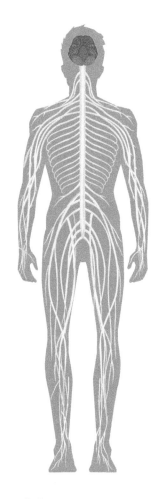

the **respiratory system**, which breathes air in and out,

the **digestive system**, which breaks down food for your cells,

the **urinary system**, which cleans liquids out of your body,

and the **nervous system**, which moves messages all around your body.

And all these systems work together to make a truly marvelous machine, your fabulous human body!

What other amazing things are there
to learn about your body?

You're a young scientist.

Go find out!

GET THE COMPLETE SET OF

39

THE FABULOUS HUMAN BODY CARDS

THE FABULOUS HUMAN BODY

CARDS

SKELETAL SYSTEM
1. Skeletal System
2. Skull
3. Teeth
4. Spine
5. Rib Cage

MUSCULAR SYSTEM
6. Muscular System
7. Biceps
8. Triceps
9. Calf Muscles
10. Achilles Tendon

CIRCULATORY SYSTEM
11. Circulatory System
12. Blood Vessels
13. Arteries
14. Veins
15. Capillaries
16. Heart

RESPIRATORY SYSTEM
17. Respiratory System
18. Windpipe
19. Bronchi
20. Lungs
21. Alveoli
22. Diaphragm

SKELETAL SYSTEM

SKELETAL S

All of your bones wo
make a system calle
system. The jobs of
system are these:

• hold your body's

• protect importa
  body

• give muscles s
  to, so you can

• make your bloo

1

2

3

Visit: heronbooks.com

Printed in the USA
CPSIA information can be obtained
at www.ICGtesting.com
CBHW041416260324
5873CB00005BA/10

THE FABULOUS HUMAN BODY
ANATOMY
for Young Scientists

Name _____ Date _____

PURPOSE
Learn what the different parts of
your body are and what they do.

HOW TO USE THIS LEARNING GUIDE: You can use this learning guide to study on your own. Just read a step, do it, and check it off. Then you can go right on to the next step!

Do each step in order without skipping around.

When you complete a section, check in with your teacher and show them your work.

A. YOUR FABULOUS MACHINE

☐ READ: *The Fabulous Human Body,* page vi, Your Young Scientist Journal.

☐ ACTIVITY: Get a *Young Scientist Journal,* a notebook you like, or make a science journal of your own. If you want, write on the inside "The Fabulous Human Body," or "Human Body Adventure" or whatever you want.

  ❏ Think of, and write down in your journal, some ways you would like to use it.

☐ READ: *The Fabulous Human Body,* Chapter 1 Your Fabulous Machine.

☐ ACTIVITY: Think of some things about the human body you are curious about. Tell another person what they are.

_____
Teacher check in

B. CELLS AND MORE

☐ READ: Chapter 2 Trillions of Living Things, section "The Smallest Part."

☐ ACTIVITY: Look at the pictures of different kinds of cells on page 4.

☐ READ: Chapter 2, section "Cells Are Alive."

☐ ACTIVITY: Lightly brush your hand or fingernail against your skin and see if you can see any dead skin cells come off.

☐ READ: Chapter 2, section "Cells Get Rid of Waste."

☐ ACTIVITY:

    ☐ In your science journal, draw a picture of a cell.

    ☐ Show the things it needs to live, and its wastes. Label what it is.

    ☐ Share your drawing with another person.

☐ READ: Chapter 2, section "Little Machine, Big Machine" to the end of the chapter.

☐ ACTIVITY: Use objects to show another person how a machine takes in fuel, uses it to move, and produces waste. Explain how your body does the same thing.

☐ READ: Chapter 3 Cells Make Tissues.

☐ ACTIVITY: Explain to another person what tissue is.

☐ READ: Chapter 4 Tissues Make Organs.

☐ ACTIVITY:

    ☐ In your journal, make a drawing that shows how cells make tissues and tissues make organs.

    ☐ Label it.

    ☐ Share your drawing with another person.

☐ READ: Chapter 5 Organs Make Systems.

☐ ACTIVITY: Use objects to show your teacher

    ☐ how your body is made up of trillions of living cells,

    ☐ which work together to make tissues,

    ☐ and tissues work together to make organs,

    ☐ and organs work together to make systems.

_____
Teacher check in

C. STAND UP!

☐ READ: Chapter 6 Stand Up!, section "Skeleton."

☐ ACTIVITY:

    ☐ Feel the bones protecting your heart and lungs. Feel how they go all the way around to your backbone.

    ☐ Feel the bone protecting your brain.

    ☐ Start with your backbone and feel your ribs all the way around to your front.

    ☐ Stand up and notice how your bones are helping you do that. Feel how they are attached to your leg muscles.

☐ READ: Chapter 6, section "Joints."

☐ ACTIVITY: Feel these joints in your body. Notice how they let you move in different directions.

    ☐ neck joint   ☐ elbow joint

    ☐ wrist joint   ☐ shoulder joint

    ☐ hip joint   ☐ knee joint

    ☐ ankle joint   ☐ toe joints

☐ ACTIVITY: Count the joints in the fingers of one of your hands. Open and close your hand and see how the joints help your fingers move and bend.

☐ READ: Chapter 6, section "Skull and Teeth" to the end of the chapter.

☐ ACTIVITY: Use a picture of a skeleton (or a skeleton model if you have one), and find each of these parts of the skeletal system:

☐ a joint ☐ skull

☐ teeth ☐ spine

☐ rib cage ☐ bones of the hands

☐ bones of the feet ☐ elbow

☐ ACTIVITY:

☐ Look at the ribs in the picture on page 29 or on a skeleton model.

☐ Find the ribs that are attached to the breastbone and notice the ones that are not attached.

☐ Now feel all these parts on yourself.

☐ ACTIVITY: Get the pack of skeletal system cards.

☐ Look through the cards until you can look at any of them and say the name of the body part and what it does without looking.

☐ Get another person to show you the card pictures one at a time, while you name each part. If you have any trouble, look at the back and continue until you know them all well.

☐ Next, have the person show you the card pictures again. This time you name each part and say what it does. (You don't have to say exactly what it says on the back of the card.) If you have any trouble, look at the back, and continue until you know them all well.

_____

Teacher check in

D. MOVE!

☐ READ: Chapter 7 Move! As you are reading, locate on your own body the muscles that are mentioned.

☐ ACTIVITY:

    ☐ Pick up something heavy with one hand and lift it by bending your arm at the elbow. With your other hand, feel your flexed biceps on the front part of your upper arm.

    ☐ Hold something heavy in one hand above your head with your arm straight. Then bend your upper arm back at the elbow so that you are holding the object behind your head. With your other hand, feel your flexed triceps on the back side of your upper arm.

☐ ACTIVITY: Use a picture (or a model of a human body if you have one), and find each of these parts of the muscular system.

    ☐ biceps   ☐ triceps

    ☐ calf muscles   ☐ Achilles tendon

☐ ACTIVITY: Get the pack of muscular system cards.

    ☐ Just like you did earlier, look through the cards until you can say the name of the body parts and what they do.

    ☐ Have another person show you the card pictures while you name each part. Continue until you know them well.

    ☐ The person shows you the cards again, and this time you name each part and say what it does, until you've got it.

_____

Teacher check in

E. THUMP THUMP!

☐ READ: Chapter 8 Thump Thump!

☐ ACTIVITY: Find some veins just under the surface of the skin by looking for some bluish or bluish-green lines on someone's hand or the inside of their wrist.

☐ ACTIVITY: Put your hand on your chest, throat, or wrist and feel your heartbeat.

☐ ACTIVITY: Find these parts of the circulatory system on a picture or model of the body.

    ☐ artery   ☐ vein

    ☐ capillaries   ☐ heart

☐ ACTIVITY: Get the pack of circulatory system cards.

    ☐ Look through the cards until you can say the name of the body parts and what they do.

    ☐ Have another person show you the card pictures while you name each part. Continue until you know them well.

    ☐ The person shows you the cards again, and this time you name each part and say what it does, until you've got it.

_____

Teacher check in

F. BREATHE!

☐ READ: Chapter 9 Breathe!

☐ ACTIVITY:

    ☐ Put your hands on your ribs and take a deep breath. Think about how your diaphragm moves downward and makes room for your lungs to fill with air.

    ☐ Keep your hands on your ribs, take another deep breath, then breathe out. Think of how your diaphragm is moving back up and pushing the air out. Feel your ribs go down.

    ☐ Do these two steps a few times.

☐ ACTIVITY: Find these parts of the respiratory system on a picture or model of the body.

    ☐ windpipe   ☐ bronchi

    ☐ bronchioles   ☐ lungs

    ☐ alveoli   ☐ diaphragm

☐ ACTIVITY: Get the pack of respiratory system cards.

    ☐ Look through the cards and practice on your own until you can say the name of the body parts and what they do.

    ☐ Have another person show you the cards while you name each part. Continue until you know them well.

    ☐ The person shows you the cards again, and you name each part and say what it does, until you've got it.

_____
Teacher check in

G. HUNGRY?

☐ READ: Chapter 10 Hungry?

☐ ACTIVITY: Chew a cracker or other bit of food to produce some saliva in your mouth. Then feel the back of your jaw with your fingers where your jawbone curves up. A little in front of that curve, but at the top of your throat, you can feel little lumps. These are two of your salivary glands.

☐ ACTIVITY: Using the picture on pages 52 and 53, or a model of a human body, find each of these parts of the digestive system.

    ☐ esophagus   ☐ stomach

    ☐ small intestine   ☐ pancreas

    ☐ liver   ☐ large intestine

    ☐ rectum

☐ ACTIVITY: Using the picture on pages 52 and 53, or a model of a human body, trace the path the food you eat follows from when you eat it until it is passed as waste. Explain to your teacher what happens to your food in each part of the digestive system.

_____
Teacher check in

H. THIRSTY?

☐ READ: Chapter 11 Thirsty?

☐ ACTIVITY: Using the picture on page 56, or a model of a human body, find these parts of the urinary system.

  ☐ kidneys   ☐ bladder

☐ ACTIVITY: Get the cards for the digestive and urinary systems.

  ☐ Look through the cards until you can say the name of the body parts, what they do, and the system they are a part of.

  ☐ Have another person show you the card pictures while you name each part and the system it is a part of. Continue until you know them well.

  ☐ The person shows you the cards again, and this time you name each part, and say what it does and its system, until you've got it.

_____

Teacher check in

I. MOVING MESSAGES

☐ READ: Chapter 12 Moving Messages.

☐ ACTIVITY: Move some part of your body. Explain to another person how your nervous system made that happen.

☐ ACTIVITY: Use your nervous system. With your eyes closed, touch several different things. Notice what you feel just by touching.

☐ ACTIVITY: Using the picture on page 60, find these parts of the nervous system.

  ☐ nerves

  ☐ brain

  ☐ spinal cord

☐ ACTIVITY: Get the pack of nervous system cards.

    ☐ Look through the cards until you can say the name of the body parts and what they do.

    ☐ Have another person show you the card pictures while you name each part and say what it does, until you've got it.

_____

Teacher check in

J. A TRULY AMAZING MACHINE

☐ READ: Chapter 13 A Truly Amazing Machine.

☐ ACTIVITY: Add some notes to your journal about what you've learned about the human body, questions you might want to explore, or anything else you want to put in your journal before you move on to the next activities.

☐ ACTIVITY: Get the pack of cards for all the systems.

    ☐ Look through the cards until you can say the name of the body parts and what they do.

    ☐ Have another person show you the card pictures while you name each part. Continue until you know them well.

    ☐ The person shows you the cards again, and this time you name each part and say what it does, until you've got it.

☐ ACTIVITY:

    ☐ Get a pack of all the cards and a piece of butcher paper that is long enough for another person to lie on.

    ☐ Remove these cards from your pack:

        ☐ skeletal system   ☐ veins

        ☐ nervous system   ☐ capillaries

        ☐ nerves   ☐ muscular system

        ☐ circulatory system   ☐ respiratory system

        ☐ blood vessels   ☐ digestive system

        ☐ arteries   ☐ urinary system

❑ Take the rest of the cards, and turn them so that the pictures are face up.

❑ Have another person lie on the butcher paper while you draw an outline of the other person's body.

❑ Use the body map attached to this learning guide to practice putting the cards on the body outline in the right places. When you can do this quickly, have another person time you. You pass when you can do it without mistakes in less than two minutes.

_____

Final Teacher check in

THE FABULOUS HUMAN BODY MAP

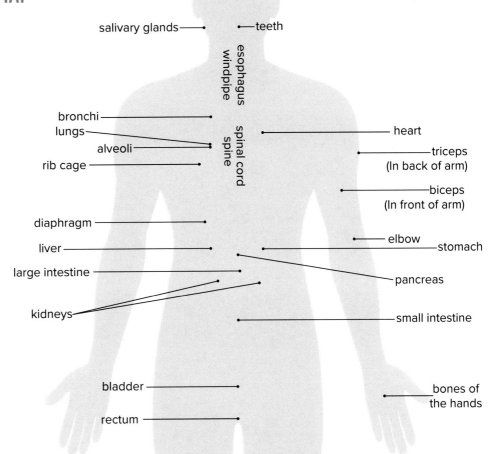

brain — skull

salivary glands — teeth

esophagus
windpipe

bronchi

lungs

alveoli

rib cage

spinal cord
spine

heart

triceps
(In back of arm)

biceps
(In front of arm)

diaphragm

liver

large intestine

kidneys

elbow — stomach

pancreas

small intestine

bladder

rectum

bones of
the hands

calf muscles
(In back of leg)

Achilles tendon
(In back of leg)

bones of
the feet

I completed

THE FABULOUS HUMAN BODY
ANATOMY
for Young Scientists

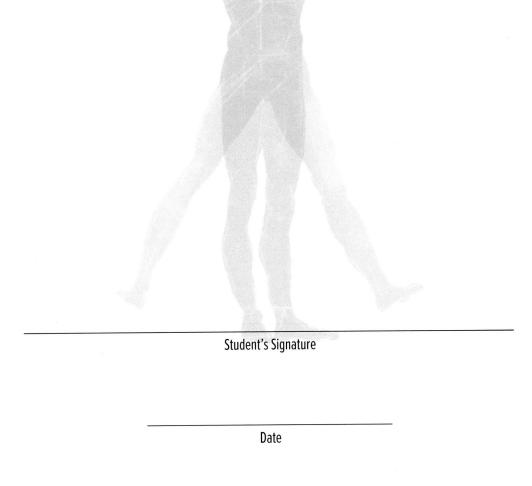

_____

Student's Signature

_____

Date